SHOCK VALUE

$HOCK VALUE

a **CAM GIRL'S**

SEXY and

HILARIOUS

STORIES of

CAPITALIZING

on **SEXUAL DESIRE**

ELIZA WILDE

Published by
Eliza Wilde, LLC
www.ElizaWilde.com

paperback ISBN: 978-0-578-52523-5

Cover and interior design by www.DominiDragoone.com
Cover images © Femme Art Boudoir, www.FemmeArtBoudoir.com
Illustrations © makegood/123rf, Paul Stringer/123rf

10 9 8 7 6 5 4 3 2 1

"When a man talks dirty to a woman,
it's sexual harassment.
When a woman talks dirty to a man,
it's $3.95 a minute."
—Unknown

I dedicate this book to my #squad, my loyal ladies,
and to all the perverted little sexual deviants
out there. Embrace your weirdness!

CONTENTS

WARNING

All the content in this book is completely original. The content, language, and scenarios may strike some readers as vulgar, offensive, controversial, indecent, or prurient. It is satire. It is not my intention to offend anyone; however, when writing this book, my intentions were to keep it as authentic as possible. Please adjust your expectations and interpretations accordingly.

I am not a real model, actress, YouTube star, or Instagram celebrity. I am an everyday, average, working, middle-class, 40-year-old, twice-divorced woman with a fur baby. I have a full-time day job that I absolutely love. I never wanted to be famous or in the limelight. I have a fear of public speaking and feel extremely uneasy on a stage or being the center of attention. I literally break out in hives and sweat like a whore in church every time I have to present a briefing in front of people. I'm not socially awkward—in fact, most people would say I am pretty outgoing and can talk to anyone. Not that I want

to, though, because in everyday circumstances, I try to avoid most people. I suppose you could label me an introverted extravert.

I grew up in a medium-sized New England town in a somewhat conservative family. I was your typical tomboy who loved to run, climb trees, ride bikes, and play sports. I was never the prom queen or the head cheerleader—instead, I was the badass jock with lots of guy friends. I was somewhat shy growing up and had one boyfriend in high school. Even in my twenties, I was never very confident in myself. I thought of myself as somewhat average on the looks scale, although some would disagree with me and tell me I'm too humble.

Be that as it may, I still lacked confidence. It wasn't until I hit my thirties and had my fair share of men that I began to have more confidence in myself. I don't know exactly what it is, but I feel that something changes in a woman's brain when she hits her late thirties or early forties. There are no fucks left to give—and hence my alter ego as a webcam girl.

You may wonder, what is a cam model or "camming"? Well, according to the illustrious Wikipedia (since an "official definition" doesn't exactly exist!), a webcam model is "a video performer who is streamed upon the internet with a live webcam broadcast. They often perform erotic acts online, such as stripping, in exchange for money, goods,

or attention." That's what I do, and I'm going to tell you all about it. And while I'm sharing my stories, I also offer some tips and suggestions for those of you interested in joining the webcamming world. Enjoy!

INTRODUCTION

A bleached asshole is nothing to laugh about, unless you read this book—then you *should* be laughing. Putting it all out there, this tale of a webcam model will entertain, enthrall, and maybe horrify you a bit.

Whatever the reaction, please know, dear reader, that this webcam model, your author, is much more than her story reveals. For most of her adult life, she served our country in the military; she has a college degree, she has loved and lost (just like most of us), and she works a full-time job as an investigator in a law firm. That's where I met her, having no idea about her other job. I am one of the attorneys who works with her at that law firm. Oh, and she's a great dog mom.

It took a lot of courage for her to reveal her secret employment to me. I was intrigued, and I knew I would support her as much as I possibly can. I realized that the shame and hesitation that anyone in her position would have in being a cam girl is simply an unfair construct of

her society. Our girl works hard and is simply trying to make a living by providing services that are obviously in great demand out there on the web.

For as advanced as we would like to think our society is, insofar as sex is concerned, forget about it. I anticipate that a lot of readers will presume that our girl is a prostitute, or significantly emotionally damaged, or has daddy issues, or whatever. So typical that we try to blame the provider rather than the customer. In reading this book, it becomes evident that the customers are the ones who are damaged— or maybe not—maybe they just have strange sexual urges or fetishes. There is a whole market out there for these customers. What is wrong with tapping into that market to make a few extra bucks? Do we always have to judge others?

Besides supplementing her income from her day job, our girl has gained a few good stories to share in the process. That's what's happening—a few, of many, good stories about the freaky things that happen online with cam girls. The sky's the limit in what they are asked to do for their clients. Some of those clients just want to talk, some of them want to be dominated, and some of them want to demonstrate how toothpaste can be used as lube. (Yes, you read that right.)

If there is anyone in this who deserves to keep her head up, it's the author. I know her to be wicked smart,

funny, insightful, and always fun to be around. As you read her story, don't judge. If you have to, judge her clients for all the crazy, funky shit they ask her to do. It kind of makes one wonder why, with such a big demand for kinky stuff, this all has to be so secretive and shameful.

This book will light you up in terms of showing what's out there in the real world, giving a glimpse into the closet of freakdom where asshole bleachery (and other fuckery) is a real thing.

Sit back, enjoy, and welcome to the webcamming world. You won't be disappointed.

—Child of Jesus

SHOCK VALUE

CHAPTER 1

THE BEGINNING

I t all started in 2017, when I was looking for a part-time job to help pay off my debt, but I couldn't find anything I was interested in doing that paid enough. As I was looking for part-time work, I thought to myself, hmmm … what kind of job can I do that doesn't require me to deal with a lot of people in person, doesn't make me work weekends if I choose not to, pays a decent wage, and doesn't run me ragged? I seriously loathe most of humanity, so the less interaction I have with them, the better. That's when I saw an ad on Craigslist for a "chat hostess" and replied.

Okay, before you get all Judge Judy on me for responding to a Craigslist ad, I contemplated for months whether or not I should respond to the ad. Thankfully, when I finally did, I realized it wasn't a hoax or scam. In fact, I discovered that it was a female-run studio. After corresponding with the studio manager via text, we met up at the studio to go over the specifics, and she created a profile for me for the website. I was concerned because

I didn't want anyone in my family or the majority of my friends to know what I was doing. But this company is very discreet—you can block up to five different states or countries.

I was 39 when I started and didn't really have any mentors, just a little training. I sat with a woman who was a seasoned cam model and worked as the manager's assistant when she wasn't doing her own camming. She would teach me how to interact with the men, how to keep them interested, and shared some things not to do, such as being on my phone all the time. When you are constantly on your phone, you appear uninterested, and guys will pick up on that. Your social media can wait—you are here to make money. She also showed me how to block customers, how to report them, and how to add little notes about them such as their names, where there are from, etc. She also suggested that every time a guy takes you exclusive or even private (two features I'll explain in more detail later), try to remember some details about the session, such as whether it involved a specific roleplay or fetish. When you click on a customer's profile name, it allows you to mark them as a favorite or add notes about them. It makes the customer feel special when you remember them by their real name if they gave it to you. If you remember their little kink or fetish or remind them about the last roleplay you did together, it *really* makes them feel

special, like you were really listening to them. Anything you can do to impress the customer will score you big points! It's a lot of improv, since men are into all kinds of crazy and wild things. I worked out of a studio for a few months, then told them I needed more flexibility and had decided to cam from home. I saved up money for a new laptop and webcam, but I still work for the company.

When camming, I am interacting with the customer, but I can also walk away from him and it won't cost me my job. I can stop my show at any time. I can block customers who are rude, mean, or make inappropriate comments to me. It is all at my discretion, and I don't put up with shit.

Men try to demand that I show them my breasts for free. Who do these guys think they're kidding? I always think, this is not YouPorn, honey—this shit is not free! It's five bucks for a tit flash, and I don't flash them quick and then put the girls away—I keep them out for a good minute or so. You come to this site knowing you have to pay, so quit being a douchebag.

My friends who know about my alter ego have asked me how I can be so brazen online. How can I expose myself to thousands of people over the internet? Aren't I nervous or scared? I really don't put too much thought into it, is what I tell them. You don't see all the people who are in your chat room—you merely see their screen

names. It makes it less intimidating, and it's easier to act like yourself without actually seeing all eyes on you. Do I worry I might know someone coming into my chat room? Sure I do, but I don't obsess over it. Considering the many thousands of models on the site I am on, and the thousands of men online looking, the likelihood of me actually knowing someone who enters my chat room is slim to none.

Now, to be fair, I must disclose that I used to be a phone sex operator back in the day. It was around 2011, and my best friend was living with me at the time. Somehow the topic of making extra money came up, and I have no idea how this idea came into my head, but I asked her, "What do you think about doing the whole 'phone sex operator' thing?" Surprisingly, she was totally for it! I researched companies, and we submitted our online applications. I will tell you, though, it is not very lucrative. I only did that job for a few months before I got bored with it. But it did make me less inhibited when I started camming, and it helped me become more vocal and creative. I did my very first humiliation roleplay while working as a phone sex operator!

The thing to remember is, this is a game. A game in which I can use my master skills of manipulation to keep them coming back for more. I like to get inside the heads of these men. I want to know what pushes their buttons.

Sometimes I think I should have studied psychology instead of law. I have worked in the legal field for about 15 years, working at various law firms as a paralegal and in prosecution, defense, and disability law. After working as a paralegal for a number of years, I changed careers. Now I am an investigator, but I still work in the legal field.

In the line of webcam work, however, having a degree in psychology would be beneficial and make camming that much more interesting. Hell, cam models need to be shrinks, girlfriends, whores, dominatrixes, the girl next door, or simply someone to watch. Being versatile, spontaneous, open-minded, and able to think on your feet are attributes that successful webcam models should have, or at least strive to have.

So many people assume that to be successful in the sex industry, you have to look a certain way physically. Let me tell you, people love variety, and screw your beauty standards! There is a body for everybody! Everyone who cams will find their own audience. You could be a 60-year-old cougar cam model and be a kinky minx and make money. You could be a pleasantly plump goddess, and because you have a kick-ass personality and are sexually adventurous, the guys will come back for more.

You see, it's not just a woman's physical assets that keep men coming back for more. I use my intellect as my weapon of choice. If I can intrigue a man based on

my personality, witty banter, intellect, and charm, then I know I have him hooked. One of the greatest compliments I have received from a customer was, "Your intelligence is so sexy, I have never been this turned on before"—and I still had all my clothes on.

At 40, never did I think I would have such a big fan base by camming only part-time. I currently have over 3,500 people who have listed me as a "favorite." I also never thought a woman my age would actually be success-ful at it, because like a lot of people out there, I assumed that most of the successful webcam models were in their early twenties with flawless skin and perfect bodies. The younger guys like me because I am their fantasy cougar. Blonde, 40, big boobs and a big booty—and of course, a lot of experience and very low inhibitions. The older men in their fifties and sixties enjoy me because I'm more on their maturity level. Of course, I'm still fun and playful, but I can hold conversations with them on various topics. The older men tend to chat more, are less demanding, and are more about eroticism.

So now that I've told you the basics, let me tell you about some of the wild adventures I've had in the business!

PRO TIP #1

Don't be afraid to explore your sexuality. Sexual acts or desires you may have found strange or weird in the past may be something you want to explore further. Reading blogs or stories about various sexual acts or kinks may be enlightening for you now. Because I work as an investigator, I am a naturally nosy person. I want to know everything about everything. Figuring out what buttons to push on a person is challenging, and what I mean by pushing buttons is what turns them on sexually.

CHAPTER 2

WTF DID I JUST READ?

I felt like such a virgin when I first started as a webcam model. Of course, I'd had plenty of sexual experiences throughout my life. I'm 40, attractive, twice divorced, and did my fair share of dating in between. Yet I literally had to do research on various sexual terms and acts, since I had never heard of them before. I guess I was considered "vanilla." When guys would request JOI (Jerk Off Instructions), CEI (Cum Eating Instructions), and cuckold, I had to ask them what on earth they were referring to. After that, I knew I had to research so I could be "in the know" with these terms and acts and so I could properly perform for them. After I did some reading, I was shocked to discover how much of a thing those acts really are, and how popular they are. Do men seriously "get off" by being told how to jerk off? Men actually get turned on by being a cuckold?

For those who are not familiar with the "cuckold" term, it is when a husband willingly encourages his wife to fuck other people because it brings him pleasure. Usually, if another man is involved, he is younger, better looking, and with a much bigger cock than the husband. A lot of times, the cuckold fantasy will coincide with SPH. SPH, aka Small Penis Humiliation, is probably one of my favorite acts to perform for my customers. Customers have actually tagged me "SPH QUEEN" and "BRUTAL SPH" on my cam profile! Yet another term I had to research, men with small cocks get pleasure when you humiliate them due to the small size of their penis. They typically request a cam-2-cam session where I accept their request to view them on their end. The more you make fun of the man's cock size, and the more creative you are with your verbiage, the better. Then they actually thank me for making them cum and for my brutality. Now tell me, Dr. Ruth, what would you have to say about this?

I always say, first impressions are lasting impressions. Men are visual creatures, and I think a lot of men appreciate when a woman puts in some effort with her appearance. Now, you may be wondering what my "den of sin" or "secret red room" looks like. Well, I for sure do not have a "secret red room" like in the movie *Fifty Shades of Grey*. Each cam model has her own personal style and set-up. I am set up in my bedroom, so I wanted to make it alluring and

enticing. I have a black-and-white-themed bedroom with a canopy bed and black canopy netting. I have candles set up and small string lights around the top of the canopy for a little extra bling. I also have numerous pillows, and I always make sure my room looks neat and presentable. And I *always* have music playing on my computer.

I try to give the same level of attention to my appearance. Some might label me as vain, and I would not disagree. However, when men come into my chat room for the first time, I want them to stay. Nine times out of ten, I am dressed in some sort of lingerie. That is just my personal preference. I like to incorporate various colors and styles, and I am a huge fan of stockings of all different colors. I actually put thought into my outfit, makeup, and hair for the days I cam because I like to keep it interesting. I have certain guys who come by to say hi just to see what I am wearing. I don't spend obscene amounts of money on my lingerie. I don't go to Victoria's Secret or any other high-end lingerie store, because it all looks the same. Amazon is a godsend! I always find pretty and inexpensive pieces of lingerie there, plus you can't beat the free two-day shipping if you are an Amazon Prime member. Guys go to a webcam model's room to fulfill some sort of fantasy. What fun is it going online to see a webcam model in an old T-shirt and some ratty shorts, her hair looking like a rat's nest? Sadly, this world bases a lot of

opinions and judgments on first impressions. That is why I always try to look my best. In my opinion, putting in effort is worth the time. Men appreciate it too, trust me! I get compliments on my room, hair, outfit, and makeup all the time. When men see you put in effort, it entices them to spend more time with you. It shows you want to impress them! The more you impress, the more lucrative it is for you!

PRO TIP #2

Don't be afraid to get creative. Be creative with anything, really; outfits, hair, room set-up. It makes you stand out and be remembered by customers. There are a few cam models who create games for their customers, which I think is cute. They create a spinning wheel or a poster board with numbers, and customers who tip can choose a number. Whoever tips the highest in a set timeframe gets a prize. Sometimes it is for a custom video the model created to sell, or custom photos to give to their customers that they would typically have to pay for. Some models wear fun wigs or costumes. Some cam models are really into cosplay, too, and the men eat it up!

CHAPTER 3

THE "NORMAL" TYPES

I didn't even know him, but the words he said to me as he was typing intrigued me. He was smart, charming, sweet, and extremely complimentary, but also a complete pervert.

It was the first time "Chris" had come into my webcam chat room. Instantaneously, he lavished me with compliments. I sat and wondered, "is this guy on something?," because right from the very start, he was enamored with me. I was completely being myself, chatting and answering questions from other men in my open chat room. I don't ever act like someone I'm not, unless I'm doing a roleplay for a customer or trying to entice someone to take me private or exclusive. I like men (and women for that matter) to see me for me. I have to be real for these people because I want them to keep coming back to me.

It's a challenge for me in some respects. I challenge myself by coming up with new and fun roleplay ideas. I buy all sorts of lingerie and outfits to keep my customers visually pleased. I challenge myself sexually with regard to how long I can hold off without touching myself and edging. It really is just a game, though—a game where I use my manipulation skills to make them want more of me.

Chris took me away to "exclusive" because he "just had to have me to himself." This is the kind of customer I *love* to have an encounter with—first, because money seems to be no object and completely disposable, and second, because they are down-to-earth, flirty, funny, charming, and engaging.

I found out that Chris lived in Georgia and worked in IT. He told me he really enjoyed getting to know the models on the site, and so he said, "Let's get to know one another, okay?" At this point, I was intrigued. I charge $5.99 per minute in my exclusive room. When a person takes me exclusive, it is just he and I. No one else can enter the room. I charge $4.99 a minute for my private shows; however, multiple people can come into my private chat room to watch. I don't do any fetishes, roleplays, or specific requests in my private chat. This is because it is difficult to perform a certain fetish for just one person when multiple guys come to my private room. In private, I typically strip, talk dirty, and use toys—vanilla stuff.

Now, what most people do not know is that the models do not keep all that money. I only make 20% of my rates. The website gets their cut, of course. And since the studio essentially recruited me, they still get their cut even though I am camming from home now. My rates are very comparable to many of the models on the site. Some have the audacity to charge $15.00 a minute. I don't know if they are delusional or if their vaginas are made out of gold, but I don't know how they even get any business. I don't raise my rates because I enjoy my regulars. They are my true bread and butter. Keep 'em cumming and coming back for more!

Chris asked me various questions, such as my interests, where I grew up, what I do for work—the norm. He was one of those men who are just easy to chat with— no real expectations, but it was fun getting to know him. He was ten years older than me, so his maturity came through, which was a nice break from dealing with 20-year-olds who want me to be their damn mother. Although he was mature, he had a good sense of humor. The words he used to describe what he wanted to do to me seriously turned me on.

"Lie back and get comfortable," he told me. I gathered some pillows around me and laid back. "Feel me caress every inch of your body. I want you to feel me worship you. I want to make you feel amazing."

I then found myself teasing him by touching myself. He was really taking his time with me, which was quite a change from the typical guys online. He truly enjoys making women feel amazing! Our conversation just flowed. He was very erotic, and I wondered if he had lots of women in his life. All of a sudden, our conversation stopped as he was kicked out of my exclusive show with a message that he needed to contact customer support. He must have gone over his daily limit. Secretly, I was disappointed because I thoroughly enjoyed chatting and flirting with him.

I got dressed again and went back to my open chat room. Next thing I knew, I saw a screen name come back to my open chat room. It looked almost identical to his screen name, and wouldn't you know it, it was him again! He told me he had to create a slightly different screen name and register a new credit card in order to take me exclusive again! I was floored.

"Dude, are you serious? You really just created a new profile just so you could continue to chat with me today?"

"Yes! I just had to!" he replied. "I couldn't get enough, and I was enjoying our time together so much!"

"Wow, I am really flattered. I can honestly say this is a first for me!"

He laughed and took me back exclusive before anyone else could take me away. I kept laughing at this situation,

mostly because I was still in shock. He had already spent hundreds. We continued chatting, and he told me about all the other cam models he had encountered and befriended. He explained that he has certain "types" he enjoys chatting with—usually women in their thirties and forties because of their maturity level, but once in a while a woman in her twenties will surprise and intrigue him. He told me that getting to know the cam models makes the experience for him so much more pleasurable because he develops a mental connection with that person. It makes him feel comfortable and allows him to be vulnerable, which can make his camming experience especially enjoyable if it is with the right person.

But this guy can make any woman feel sexy with his words alone. We both ended up climaxing, and this time, I didn't have to fake it! We say our goodbyes, and he assured me that he would be back again soon.

Truth be told, I was ready for a break. I really had to work my vagina into overtime that week. Both the website and the studio I work for had bonuses that week. Models had to stream for 25 hours from Saturday to Saturday to be eligible for the bonus money. And when I say stream, that means active streaming. That doesn't include pause times or breaks. If you streamed for 25 hours and made $250.00 that week, the website *and* studio would add $25.00 to your earnings. If you made $500.00 in the week,

they would each add $50.00, and if you earned $1,000.00, they would each add $100.00 to your earnings. Then there was an additional bonus where if you placed within the top 200 models, you could get more bonus money. The first prize was $5,000! The lowest a model could make in bonus money was $200.00.

In the end, I placed 118th out of 200, so I made that extra $200.00—and since I made over $1,000 that week, I would get an additional $200.00. I was meticulous as to narrowing down which days I would cam and for how long. I tracked my minutes very closely because it is exhausting working a full-time job, getting in my gym time, and taking care of whatever else I need to get done. Adulting sucks.

Oh, and to top it off, I knew I was getting my fucking period that Friday, so I had to cram in my 25 hours between Saturday night and Thursday night! Of course I could cam on my period, but I would be cramping, bloated, and downright pissy with those men. There are some simple tricks for a model to cam while on her period, and I've used them when I was desperate for some cash. What I personally do is cut my tampon string super short where it doesn't show. One time I felt like I was digging for gold because I cut the string so short! I thought to myself, "This is it. This is my embarrassing emergency room story where I can't get my fucking tampon out and

a doc has to get on up there and find it!" At least that way, I can still play with myself but not insert any toys. A lot of models, myself included, just tell the guys that there is no pussy fucking for the day. I usually lie and say I got fucked super hard by my boyfriend multiple times and am really sore. They usually don't care and would rather me tell my story in detail to them!

I honestly don't know how the women who cam full-time do it. My vagina was beat up. These men wanted all the pussy-pounding they could get. Jesus, not even my best sloppy blow job satisfied them. Thankfully, on Wednesday night, one of my favorite long-time regulars came by my chat room to pay me a long-overdue visit.

Max was his name. We had kept in touch via email over the past year. He is a physician from Pennsylvania and very easy to talk to. The very first day he came to my chat room, he took me exclusive for about an hour. Not once did he tell me he wanted me to strip down, talk dirty, or do whatever else would get him off. He literally just chatted with me. We talked about our day jobs, where we were from, our interests, etc. He has a great sense of humor, and our conversation just flows.

He is one of the customers who is turned on by my personality. He does pay me compliments on my phys-ical appearance, but he appreciates my sense of humor and intelligence. It had been many months since he had

logged on to the website. He said he got bored of it and needed to take a break. Maybe I was wiping out his bank account—ha!

He hit me up via email and told me he had seen me log on to the site. I told him that I was hustling, camming that week for the contest, so he told me he would make it a point to log on. Plus, he was on the West Coast for a conference, so we were actually in the same time zone, which would make it easier. But I was exhausted by the time Wednesday rolled around. I had gotten home from work and went straight to my room to rest for a while. A few hours later, I felt like garbage but remembered I had bought some Monster energy drinks, knowing I would need them that week. After drinking half of one, I emailed Max to let him know I was ready to come online.

Sure as shit, a minute after I logged on, he was there. He took me exclusive for a little over an hour. We had a lot to catch up on! We often talk about our jobs, and with him being in the medical field and me in the legal field, we have had our fair share of dealings with some strange people.

One story I will never forget him telling me happened on a New Year's Eve a few years ago. He told me he was on call that night and a man had come into the emergency room complaining of severe stomach pains. Well, after the patient had X-rays done, it was discovered that he had

shoved an entire shampoo bottle up his rectum. (You can't make this stuff up!) The man told his physician that he was at a New Year's Eve party and passed out. Allegedly, hours later he woke up with this shampoo bottle up his rectum.

Now, that is something that does not magically happen in five minutes. Max said this is something that the patient has to have been doing for quite a long time, because nobody's sphincter muscles are that loose unless this is something that has been going on for a hot minute. The patient was either in denial, or extremely embarrassed and did not want to confess to this act. Different strokes for different folks, but that one was a doozy!

The next morning, I woke up to an email from Max. He told me that I put him in such a good mood, and despite him being so exhausted with listening to lectures and workshops, he was glad he came online to see me. He proceeded to tell me how incredibly sweet and genuine I am, and that I made him forget about some of the stressors in his life. It made me feel really good that I could do that for someone.

PRO TIP #3

It is okay to be vulnerable sometimes with certain customers. After camming for some time, you will have your regulars. You will get to know them, and they will get to know you. It is normal. Men need an emotional connection too, not just women. Some of these guys are lonely or bored in their relationships, so they come online. You don't have to tell them all the details about you and your life, but just talking and flirting with them can make all the difference in the world. Sometimes men just want to talk and don't have an outlet. Just don't get too sucked in. Keep some kind of barrier up and don't divulge too much personal information. When in doubt ... lie, but keep it believable! Don't tell them that you are a flight attendant as your day job if you know nothing about it. Some guys love to ask lots of questions about you, so be prepared.

CHAPTER 4

THE SUBMISSIVES

Learning about so many kinks and fetishes is rather intriguing. I can't even begin to talk about how much I have heard and seen within the year I have been camming. One of my sweetest regulars is known as Ed. He gets notified when I come online and always makes it a point to say hello, even if it's just for a few minutes. He rarely ever takes me private or exclusive, though. Instead, he buys me stockings. He has a stocking fetish, among others. As a cam model, having an Amazon wish list can come in handy. Sometimes you have customers who are kind enough to buy you things from your list. Ed has bought me quite a few pairs of thigh-high stockings.

Now, brace yourselves, as this may be disturbing to some readers, and don't say I didn't warn you. One day, as we were chatting online, he told me he wanted my

boyfriend to cum on my stockings, and he wanted to lick the cum off of them, and he would pay me for those used stockings. I sat there stunned, as I had never heard of such a thing. So I sat and thought about it.

At the time, my boyfriend didn't know I cammed, but more on that later. I had to think quickly, so I reached out to a fellow cam model, Scott. Scott is a male cam model who considers himself bisexual. He came into my open chat room one day, and we hit it off. We started chatting, and he told me to contact him if I ever needed advice or tips. He then gave me his email so we could keep in touch. As time went on, we would hit each other up for camming tips or just to check in and say hi.

Since my boyfriend wasn't aware of my SPH Queen alter ego, I reached out to Scott to ask him if he could cum on some of my used stockings if I sent them to him. Of course, he was happy to help me out. So I gathered two pairs of old thigh-high stockings and sent them to Scott, and the following week he sent them back. I took them out of the plastic bags he had put them in, put them in a large manila envelope, and sent them off to Ed.

He was beyond excited when he received them in the mail! Naturally, he had to do a cam-2-cam session with me to show me. He then proceeded to lick all of Scott's cum off the stockings and shoved the stockings in his mouth. I sat there in awe as he licked away and shoved

them in his mouth. He was so delighted. It was like a train wreck, and I couldn't look away.

Ed sent me some other stockings; however, they were not the kind that stay up by themselves, nor did they fit over my thighs. That's what I get for being a runner. He said he would love it if I sprayed some of my favorite perfume on them and sent them to him, so that is what I did. Since I couldn't wear them, hell, someone should get some use out of them. I decided to spray some of my favorite perfume that I got while I was in Doha, Qatar. The perfumes there, or anywhere in the Middle East for that matter, are potent, and even a little bit of the scent stays on for quite a long time. They don't water down their fragrances like those in many other countries. Ed emailed me a few days later to let me know he had received the perfumed stockings, and that he slept with them under his pillow and loved waking up to my scent. Glad I made Ed's day.

"Tiff" is one of my favorite femdom boys who visits me in my chat room from time to time. For those who are not familiar what "femdom" is, it is female domination: a woman who dominates men, uses humiliation, and essentially makes her men slaves in the wonderful world of BDSM. This includes things such as face-sitting, using a leash and collar, whipping/spanking, penetration with a strap-on, making the men dress up in women's clothing or

lingerie—you get the picture. So Tiff enjoys it when we roleplay and I take him on "adventures."

Now, with Tiff, I don't need to strip down or do anything sexual during our roleplays. He just enjoys the adventures I take him on. When I talk about "adventures," I am merely speaking to him and telling him verbally what we would do. I never, ever meet up with any of the customers in person. Number one, it is not allowed, and number two, I watch far too many episodes of *Forensic Files* to ever meet up with one of these guys. I know what kind of shit goes down. I work with crazy on a daily basis.

One adventure he particularly enjoyed was when I brought him to a sex shop with a glory hole area. I told him we would need some supplies, in the form of a ball gag, nipple clamps, and a butt plug. I told him the ball gag was to shut him up when he was experiencing any amount of pleasure, as I did not allow him to moan or talk. The butt plug would strictly be for my entertainment because I would choose one that had a unicorn tail attached to it. I would make him put the plug up his ass and prance around the sex shop like a little sissy unicorn. The nipple clamps I would use to pull him around or if he got out of line.

After I was done prancing Tiff around the sex shop for everyone to see and laugh at, I brought him to the glory hole room. Now, this little fellow had no clue what a

glory hole is. In case you are not familiar with glory holes, it is slang for a slot or hole in a wall that a man sticks his cock through for sexual gratification by an anonymous person on the opposite side (think about the movie *The Sweetest Thing*, and if you've never seen it, shame on you! Great chick flick with a glory hole scene—it's not offensive, more so hilarious).

I don't have personal experience with this, but friends of mine do. Such activities are common in the gay male community. If you are there to "give," you would put your finger through the hole and rub it along the bottom. This is the common signal letting the person on the other side know you are ready to give. If you are there to "receive," just wait for the same signal. The common cue to notify the "receiver" of ejaculation is a few light taps on the wall.

I asked Tiff, "Are you ready for this?" He replied, "Oh yes, mistress, so ready!"

I took off his ball gag for the time being, and I told him to get down on his knees and give the guy on the other side the signal. A few seconds later, a big black cock, aka BBC, emerged through the hole. Tiff gasped with excitement, and I said, "Well, it's not gonna suck itself, bitch, so get to sucking!"

"Yes, mistress," he said. In the meantime, I degraded him, calling him names and telling him to gag on that BBC. I yanked down on his nipple clamps because he

wasn't sucking it good enough. He cried out in agony and pleasure simultaneously. I told him to shut the fuck up and be a good little slut and make that BBC cum. In a minute, that BBC shot his load all over Tiff's mouth and face.

I told him he had better clean it all up or he would get whipped hard. We can't leave a room messy with cum everywhere; that is not good etiquette. Tiff did a good job cleaning up the mess. I put his ball gag back in, took out his fancy unicorn tail butt plug, and told him, "For being such a good slave for your mistress, you will now take that BBC up the ass."

"Oh, thank you, mistress, I was hoping you would say that!"

The signal came from the other side of the wall, and I told Tiff to bend the fuck over and take it! He did so with such enthusiasm. I continued to degrade him, calling him a pathetic whore who secretly loves to get ass-fucked by a BBC. Of course, he agreed with me and continued to take a pounding. After our session was done, he thanked me profusely and told me he looked forward to our next "adventure."

PRO TIP #4

Keep an open mind. People have fetishes that are really fucking weird, but it's what works for them. I used to think interacting and camming for femboys was totally out there, but then I read more on the subject and it intrigued me. Most of the femboys are the sweetest guys! They love to please you when you are dominating them. As it turns out, I really enjoy dominating these guys. They are down for anything, and the more creative you are, the better—and they will tell you! Useful tip: research and read. It will really help you understand and will better prepare you to interact with these guys.

CHAPTER 5

THE NEEDY TYPE

There are some days I know I need to cam to pay the bills, but it is just so hard to find the motivation to deal with these men. I have to mentally prepare myself. I sometimes need a cocktail or two as well. It's the needy guys who drive me crazy. They just can't settle for me sucking on a dildo simulating a blow job and some dirty talk, or even a little strip tease. Hell, even a frickin' role-play is better than the needy guys.

What I mean by "needy" is that they want you to do a whole assortment of things during the show, changing it up constantly. It could be changing into a completely different outfit(s) or moving to various rooms in the house. Sometimes they want you to fuck yourself so they can see your ass, then position yourself so you are looking at them; then they want a blow job, and then they want you

to act this way or that way. It can become exhausting for just one show.

One needy customer, "Big Tom," is that way. I have a laptop with my webcam attached on top. The computer sits on a very small and lightweight table that is portable, so it can be taken apart in 20 seconds. He wanted to see me ride a toy, but riding the toy on my bed just wasn't good enough for him. He wanted me to take off everything but my thigh-high stockings and to wear my highest heels. He then wanted to see me fuck myself with my white dildo on my bathroom floor.

I positioned my laptop and table so he could see me. Well, after a minute or two of fucking myself with this thing, he wanted me to sit on my bathroom counter to watch me ride the dildo, but he wanted to see all of me. My camera doesn't have a remote to zoom in or out, so I was trying to fit my whole self in front. Meanwhile, I had one leg dangling from the bathroom counter, one leg bent up, and my vag on full display, all while trying not to have my ass fall into my damn sink.

After a few more minutes of that, he wanted me in my living room. I told him my living room does not have good lighting because I have no overhead light and very dim lamps on my tables. I do have lighting in my dining area since it's an open-concept layout. He wanted me to get on my couch and continue to ride the toy. I took the

laptop off the portable table and placed it on my coffee table in front of my couch. The lighting sucked big time, of course—I already explained this to him. He had me try various positions, and I began to get annoyed. I kept thinking to myself, "Jesus, man, will you make up your fucking mind here? This is ridiculous!," but I pressed on because I needed to hustle for this money.

Finally, he agreed with me that the lighting wasn't that great and that I should move back into the bedroom where I originally started. "Thank God," I thought. At least on my bed, I'm comfortable, and not on my couch looking like a damn contortionist!

I finally got him off, and I was just so over this whole thing. I was bored throughout the entire session. He barely said five words beyond telling me to move around all over the place. Here I was trying to talk dirty, asking him if he's stroking his cock for me, if he likes watching me fuck my pussy, etc., and I could barely get half a sentence out of him. I understand that while a guy is watching me and yanking his cock, it may be difficult to type—but come on, man, I get lots of guys having full-blown conversations with me while they're jerking off. Not every cam session will be great, so it's just the luck of the draw with whomever takes you private or exclusive. After that session, I needed a long break, so I drank myself stupid in order to continue my night.

PRO TIP #5

Stand your ground. If you are not comfortable doing certain acts after a guy takes you private or exclusive, you are not required to finish the show. You, as the cam model, can stop a show whenever you want. You do not owe these men anything! Granted, you are there for entertainment purposes—however, you do not have to give up your personal morals just to make a couple of bucks. Don't be afraid to be vocal and honest with what you will and won't do. Some guys will try and push you or manipulate you. Don't fall for it. Chances are, there is a cam model willing and able to perform whatever act(s) he wants, and you don't have to stress about appeasing a guy by doing something you truly don't want to do.

CHAPTER 6

THE BOYFRIEND

took an entire week off from camming. The week of the bonus contest essentially made my vagina crawl up inside my body completely and not want to be bothered, like a damn snail. My vagina was officially on strike. It was as though the men during that week sucked the soul right out of the poor girl. I had too many things to do every day after work anyway, and I was burnt out.

I sat at work thinking about when I would cam next. I was headed to Vegas the following weekend to visit my boyfriend at the time. We had been doing the whole long-distance thing for over a year. It was difficult at times because I had days when I just needed a long hug from him or to cuddle on the couch with him while watching some silly movie. He lived on the East Coast and I'm on the West Coast, so we decided that this visit

should be in Vegas since we'd been talking about it for quite some time.

That week I had to cam for at least three days to make some money for Vegas. I always like to have a little extra spending money, because you never know, especially since it's Vegas. Ugh, the thought of having to really put in work over the weekend sucked, but I just looked at it like these men were paying for my vacation!

The boyfriend (BF) and I had a night where we consumed a little too much alcohol, and that is when I told him about my alter ego as the "SPH Queen." It was so hard for me to keep a secret from him, and it was killing me! He knew of my phone sex operator days and thought it was hot that I'd done that job, so I figured he was pretty open-minded and wouldn't get all butt-hurt about me camming. He thought it was awesome but found my stories bizarre. I told him that everyone has their own secret fantasies or fetishes, and they can come online and express their bizarre desires without getting judged. Well, I judge them in my head, but I act enthused about performing their weird roleplay or fetish. While I'm performing these odd or bizarre fetishes, I'm thinking to myself, "Holy hell, where did you come up with this shit? This stuff really turns you on? My God, am I vanilla!" The BF also expressed interest in watching me interact with the men while I cammed. We never got around to

that, but I know I would have felt a little self-conscious about him sitting there watching me.

My BF was no secret to these guys. They often asked about him, when I would get laid next, and what our sex life was like. Some even said they would love to watch the both of us on cam in an exclusive show. I'm not sure if he would have been willing do that, but I wouldn't be opposed to it if the customer paid for a block session. A block session is when the customer pays for a committed amount of time with me. I too am committed on my end to stream for the entire time block, or I could face a suspension if I end the show early. Of course, there are exceptions when I can shut down my block session before the time is up, such as if the customer is being rude or disrespectful, or if he wants to engage in illegal activities such as incest, bestiality, etc.

The customer gets a discounted rate if they request a block session. Sessions are either 15, 30, 45, or 60 minutes long. The longer the session, the bigger the discount the customer gets. I really enjoy block sessions because I know the customer is committed and not just a 30-second flake who turns out to be a waste of my time.

Those are seriously the worst. These cheap-ass men take me private or exclusive, want me to strip, and as soon as the top comes off, or as soon as I'm completely naked, they leave my room. I mean, seriously, sometimes

my outfits are an ass-pain to get on and off, such as a cor-set. Those jerk-offs are better off scoping out some free porn than making me waste my time. Some people say it's because I get them to cum so quickly. Well, I don't know if I do or not, but it's not necessarily the case—they could be cheap asses who just want to see my tits. Hell, if that's the case, just ask for a tit flash while in open chat, and it will cost you five bucks and less of my time wasted.

The relationship with the BF did not work out—shocker—but at least I dated someone who was very open-minded and fully supported me camming. For me, at this stage in my life, it is important that I feel comfortable with my significant other knowing everything about me. I don't want to feel like I need to keep this part of my life a secret from men anymore. I need to be with someone who doesn't judge me for my side job and accepts me completely. Surprisingly enough, the men who I am just friends with seem very accepting of my webcamming—so I remain hopeful!

PRO TIP #6

Be engaging! Sitting there just staring at the camera or playing on your phone will not make you money. Welcome the guys into your open chat room when they enter. There are always new men coming onto the site, and they are unfamiliar with the world of webcamming. Try to make them feel at ease. Ask where they are from, how their day was, and keep it simple. When men see women smiling, laughing, and flirting, they see you as being a fun one to take private or exclusive, and that is your goal!

CHAPTER 7

ODD FETISHES

Fetishes are like the big box of Crayola crayons you get as a kid. There is one color in that box that you love, and there are lots to choose from, so you're bound to find something. Let's be honest—I'm sure there are a few fetishes out there that turn you on, but you'd be embarrassed to tell someone or to actually act them out.

I am one of those cam girls who, for the most part, is pretty open-minded. I do have some exceptions. Under no circumstance will I be your mommy. I will not partake in mommy/son roleplays. Number one, I am not a mother; I never wanted to be. Number two, seriously, what kind of mommy issues does one need to have for them to want me to play their mommy? I get that it is a roleplay, but it is not one that I find sexy or even remotely fun.

I mean, the look on my face when guys call me "mommy" is priceless. I have no poker face and wear my expressions for the world to see. I think it's weird and creepy, and the last thing I want to do is speak baby talk to you or spank you. I hate it when guys come into my chat room, see my age, and automatically say, "Hi, Mommy!" My response: "Do NOT call me Mommy, ever. I will NOT be your mommy, so you might as well leave my chat room now. I will, however, play your corrupt step-mommy." Sometimes guys will stick around if I tell them that, while others will leave with the hopes of finding their "mommy" to have fun with. The whole taboo step-mother roleplay is actually a big hit. Most guys in their early twenties enjoy that roleplay, and I personally think it's fun.

On one particular day, a customer by the name of "J" came by my open chat room. He asked me, of all things, if I could burp on command. Well, being the tomboy I was growing up, I learned how to burp very loudly and on command just by inhaling a lot of air. Shout-out to my childhood friend for teaching me this—I am now using this talent to make money!

Now, this actually shocked J and excited him very much. He told me he wanted to hear me burp prior to him taking me away for an exclusive one-on-one show, so I told him to take me private really quick so I could show him. Meanwhile, I was thinking to myself, "WTF

is going on right now? Is this guy actually going to get his cock hard and get off while I burp? How is this an actual thing?"

J took me private, and I let a loud burp rip. "Oh my God, you are amazing!" he replied, and then took me exclusive. He also asked if I could flex my boobs, to which I replied, "Why yes, I can!" Essentially all J wanted to do was converse and listen to me burp while I boob-flexed. *Okay, this is easy enough—strange, but easy,* I thought to myself.

"Can you burp words?" he asked. "Of course I can," I replied. So after burping some random words, J wrote, "OMG I am so hard right now." I, of course, laughed out loud, as I had no other reaction, and I just shook my head. "Ur the best belcher, I wish I had a GF like you," he wrote. Again, I laughed. "Can you burp the alphabet?" he asked. "I can. I don't know how far into the alphabet I can get, but I will give it my best shot," I told him. J was so intrigued with the loudness and length of my burps.

"You should go into another room and burp to see if I can hear you," he told me.

"Okay, let me go into my living room and I will belt one out for you." I walked out of my bedroom into my living room, went to the farthest corner, and belted out a solid belch. I went back to my bedroom and looked at my computer screen.

"Holy shit! I heard you, and heard you really good!" J exclaimed. I just laughed. "Is there another room you can go to and burp again?"

"How about I go into my walk-in closet? I have to go through my bathroom to get to my walk-in. I could close my bathroom door, and then close my closet door and burp in there," I told him.

"Oh shit, yes! That would be awesome. Let's try it!"

So I went into my bathroom, closed the door, then walked back to my walk-in and let one rip! A really long burp that came from deep down in my gut. Meanwhile, I could only think, *my walls are so fucking thin in my apartment, my neighbors are probably having a field day if they are listening.* I imagined the neighbors thinking that all this ruckus had to be coming from a 300-pound man scratching his balls and wearing a mustard-stained wife-beater two sizes too small while watching football. *Haha, little do they know!* I walked back to my bedroom and sat on my bed to read what J wrote.

"You are my new favorite! You are amazing and put me to shame," he said.

I thanked him and giggled, while I thought, "How does a guy get turned on by watching a girl belch like a man?" J then told me that he just "got off," thanked me for our session, and told me that he is looking forward to seeing me again. Of course, after our session, I had

to Google "burping fetish," and sure as shit, it is a thing. There are actual websites and forums for burp fetishes. Apparently the burp fetish forum is also a source of moral support and advice for people with a fetish that is rare and misunderstood.

In one article I read on a burping blog, a professor who is an expert in obsessive behaviors stated that "burping is one of the strangest and perhaps one of the least commonplace fetishes" that he has come across. He also went on to say, "The 'loudness' aspect appears to be an important element to burp fetishes," and that "the noise made, rather than the action itself, is what is sexualized and/or interpreted by the fetish as sexually pleasurable and arousing." Hey, whatever floats your boat, as long as you're not hurting yourself or anyone else!

PRO TIP #7

Don't be afraid to try something new, despite how strange it sounds. Sometimes you will surprise yourself and actually enjoy it. Whether it be a new sex position, sex toy, fetish, or roleplay, give it a try! Variety is the spice of life. You may discover something about yourself that you never knew you had in you.

CHAPTER 8

THE EXTREME AND IMAGINATIVE ROLEPLAY

Once in a while, you get a guy who is really into role-play—and I mean *really* into it. A guy with the screen name "SciFi" came into my open chat room to tell me he had sent me a private message about a roleplay idea. "I will check it out when I'm on a break," I told him. About ten minutes later, I went to my inbox on the site and saw his message. I am all about fun and creativity, but this took roleplaying to a whole different level. The subject line was "a wild role play," and instantly I thought, "For fuck's sake, here we go."

He started out, "Hope you are doing well. Welcome back, it's been a long time since I have seen you online. Hope you miss our wild roleplays we have done in the past." Now, mind you, I had *no* idea who this guy was unless he

had changed his screen name. I knew for a fact that we had never done *any* roleplays, because when a customer enters your free chat room, and they have spent money on you, there is a number next to their name. It will be a number from 1 to 4. The higher the number, the more money the guy has spent on you. You can also view the customer's profile to see when and how long your last private or exclusive session was. So for this guy to write about our previous "wild roleplays" was absurd, but I digress.

SciFi continued his roleplay story. "Could you imagine a roleplay like this? Assume you are a professional contract killer who kills for money, one of the best, who has killed thousands of men by using your perfect body, and never failed before. When you are killing a man, you usually fuck him first. Your favorite position is to fuck on top because you always want to control the men. You always shoot them with 44 hot lead bullets inside their body. Blood comes out everywhere—it makes you excited, and you continue to shoot and fuck them. Finally, you put your last bullets inside their mouth to finish their life. This is you, a great, sexy, professional killer!"

As I read this, I thought, "Is this guy like one of those 40-year-old weirdos who still lives in his mother's basement, drinks Mountain Dew Code Red, and has pictures of Ted Bundy and Jeffrey Dahmer taped up like they are his heroes?"

And here is the actual storyline he had come up with. "In this mission, someone hired you to kill me, and they offered you a large amount of money that you cannot refuse. At the beginning of the roleplay, as you always do before each kill, you make a recording, talk about your life as a contract killer who kills for a living, and talk about your next target. Then you go to my house to fuck me, but you are actually a professional contract killer— you are hired to kill me. Assume I am a powerful guy with a big crew. You fuck me first, then use two guns to shoot me to death. After that, my crew comes in and you are shot to death (shake your body as if being shot by 20 machine guns at the same time, so this is very intense). And here is your sad ending: an evil, greedy professional contract killer who finally got what she deserved. At the end of the roleplay (after you have killed me), please use red lipstick to put lots of red dots on your tits and stomach and make them look like bullet holes in your body." And lo and behold, the guy had attached a picture of some naked chick with all this red stuff on her that looked like paint.

After reading this, I thought, "Wow … just wow. At least he doesn't lack imagination, but this is so not worth my time." I entered my open chat room again, and SciFi came back in. I politely declined his offer. The last thing I wanted to do was get red lipstick all over my white

comforter. He said he would take me away exclusive in a 30-minute block session, but to make roughly 40 bucks for this, it wasn't worth my time. I can't get into that weirdo type of roleplay. What happened to good, old-fashioned cougar or bad teacher roleplays? The simple kind that don't require me to think too much? Thankfully, creative and elaborate roleplays such as this don't come around very often.

PRO TIP #8

Be honest about your limits. When a customer approaches you about a roleplay, sex act, or fetish they are into, and it is something you are not interested in acting out, are repulsed by, or are just uncomfortable with, try to politely decline. Guys come online to act out their fantasies that may be really strange, and I suspect some of them feel a little vulnerable. I don't want to make them feel bad or guilty, so I typically say, "I'm sorry, I really can't get into a roleplay like that," or "that really isn't my thing, and I don't want to disappoint you." Nine times out of ten, they will say, "okay, thank you," and leave your chat room. Once in a while a guy will try and beg, but I don't feed into it, and they eventually leave.

CHAPTER 9

PUT ON A HAPPY FACE

've discovered that my acting skills have become much better since I've started camming. When a guy suggests a roleplay idea or says he wants a cam-2-cam session, acting enthused and excited is almost a sure way for him to take you private or exclusive. "Oh wow, I would love to see your big cock! That would get me so excited to watch you jerk off for me!" or "Oh yes! That is my favorite roleplay—I hope you can get me off!" are typical responses.

Guys are all about showing you their cock, too, like they are just so proud of their member. They love to tell me how long they have been edging and how much cum they have stored up. "I have a huge load just for you, do you want to see how much?" "Oh my God, yes!! That would be so hot!" is my usual response, with wide eyes

and a big grin. You have to act impressed, tell them how much you like it, and how you love to watch them stroke it for you. The more "into it" you come across, the better it is for you in the long run. The guys will remember how fun you were, and how excited you were to see their throbbing member, so they will stay in your private or exclusive room longer, mark you as a favorite, and keep coming back.

Does it do anything for me to watch a guy shoot his load all over himself or a desk? Not so much. At the end of the session, I just roll my eyes and I'm on to the next show. The best are the tiny baby dicks to make fun of. Guys who are into SPH are also into exhibitionism, oddly enough. I think that, number one, it helps the model perform more brutal SPH when she can actually see the pathetic size of the cock. Number two, I think the guy loves the sheer "wow factor" when the model sees how small the cock is upon first glance.

Guys see their dicks as a trophy of some sort. Positive reinforcement is key. It really is simple psychology when dealing with the majority of these men. On top of guys wanting to show me their dicks during a cam-2-cam session, I get a rather vast amount of unsolicited dick pics sent to my private inbox. Needless to say, I am not impressed. Sure, I've seen some 11-inch cocks make their way to my inbox, but quite frankly, an 11-inch cock scares

me. I would not let that horse cock anywhere near me in person. But there are some people out there who don't mind a little pain, and I use the word "little" loosely.

Do men actually think we get turned on by a dick pic, though? I wonder if they seriously think that looking at it would make me excited to rub one out or something. Maybe for some women out there, they love a good dick pic, but for myself and the majority of women I know, not so much. Dick pics are the human equivalent of a cat giving you a dead bird as a "gift."

There are days when I am just not in the mood to entertain. Here come those acting skills again. Your persona comes across while you are online, and open chat is a big deal. A lot of guys want to see your personality shine through, or what is perceived to be your personality based on your acting abilities. A great mood needs to shine on the screen for the guys to be interested in taking you private or exclusive. They don't want to spend their money on women who won't interact with them or who come across as Debbie Downers.

If I know I'll be in a rotten mood all day, I just skip camming that day altogether. Most times, after I shower, down a Monster, and take a few sips of a cocktail, I am magically cured and good to go! I have even gone online to go into some of the other models' open chats to see what they do and to get some pointers. Some of them

just sit there and don't talk. Others are too busy on their phones—not ideal if you want to make money. Men feel like you are ignoring them or have more important things to do online than to strike up a conversation with them. I am guilty of checking my text messages, but I won't look at social media for hours because, most times, I will have numerous men in my room asking me all sorts of questions. I like to be engaged and to keep things interesting to prevent me from getting bored. Some days, if I get too bored or there isn't enough traffic in my room, I log off for a few hours and then go back.

Every model has her limits. Some women feel like they have to succumb to a man's demands for what they want. I say to hell with that nonsense. This is *my* chat room, so I will do whatever I please. I make it clear to most of the people who enter my room what I will and won't do in my shows. Most men are lazy and don't take the time to read everything about me in my profile—what my turns-on are, what I will not do, my kinks or fetishes, etc. They will usually ask what my show entails, so I give them a simple breakdown of the things I won't do. It is a shorter list. I've told men to go fuck themselves when they ask me to do something I am not willing to do while in the middle of a show. Then some of them get butt-hurt about it or simply leave my room.

I don't get offended. I figure, with all the models on this website alone, they will find someone who will do what they want. I'm not desperate enough for a couple bucks to do something I am against. I think some of the models get desperate, though, if they aren't making money, and they feel like they need to do everything the guy wants. Some men can be degrading—probably because they got picked last for dodgeball in middle school and got made fun of by the head cheerleader, so now they have to take out their aggressions on a cam model. Once a guy comes into my open chat room and observes my personality, most come to the realization that I am not a woman to be fucked with.

PRO TIP #9

Get yourself an Amazon wish list! Often men will ask me
if I have a certain item of clothing or lingerie. Sometimes
I have it, sometimes I don't. I let them know I have a wish
list if they would like to send me something
and I can message them my Amazon link.
Of course, it is linked with my model name,
not my actual name. They also don't see
my address when they buy something
from my list. They can only see the city it
is being shipped to. You can kill two birds
with one stone. You get something new
and sexy to wear, and you are satisfying
him by wearing it for him when you cam!
Sometimes, they will tip me at the end of
a show to let me know I can use their tip
to buy something nice for myself.

CHAPTER 10

EMPOWERED

A lot of you are probably wondering, what sort of people spend that kind of money to have an orgasm virtually? Well, all kinds of people! A lot of men enjoy the personal experience. They can essentially find a "custom" girl who fits their needs—a girl who fits their definition of beautiful and who fits their sexual desires, fetishes, kinks, etc. Sure, watching a video on PornHub is free, but these guys want specifics and enjoy the interaction that they can't get by merely jerking off to a video.

A lot of guys are missing that mental and emotional connection as well. Some have been married for years, but don't have sex with their wives anymore for various reasons. Some are so socially awkward that their dating life does not exist. Some work too much to have a relationship, so they get their rocks off coming online to chat with their favorite beauty. A lot of men think coming online and being intimate with a virtual stranger isn't cheating, and in some relationships, maybe it isn't. Some men find

it too risky to cheat on their wives in person, so coming online to have an orgasm with their favorite cam girl is safer. No STDs, no risk of anyone actually catching you in person, and less drama.

Besides, they can hide behind their computers or phones, and let's face it, you don't really *want* to see who is sitting behind that phone or computer. I've seen the good, the bad, and the downright ugly, but I have to maintain my enthusiasm if they decide to request a cam-2-cam session. I've had to work on my poker face a lot! There have been times I would be performing, and in the middle of my show, the guy requests a cam-2-cam session (which I always accept), and I see a 400-pound man tugging at his tiny pecker that is barely visible due to his ginormous gut hanging down. Now, for most people, that could be a shock, as it certainly was for me the first time I saw it, but now I sort of see right through them and try not to look directly at them. Thankfully, I can minimize my screen, so their picture appears much smaller on my end.

I've had guys take me exclusive when their wives or girlfriends are right next to them or sleeping close by. Those are actually pretty fun, because I find it amusing that a guy would be so ballsy as to whip out his dick, being so close to his woman, and I find myself getting enthusiastic with them. I do it because it is a power trip for me. Knowing that these guys would rather pay me to get off

than to have sex with a live person is such a rush. It turns me into a bit of a narcissist when I am performing for them because they are getting off with me instead!

Some of my friends, mainly women who are aware of my camming job, ask how I can find it in me to act or say certain things to these men, especially if they are into SPH or humiliation, denial, torture, etc. I tell them that, in fact, it is quite easy. "Have you ever been so fucked over by a man, or numerous men, that you end up in a dark place and loathe men altogether?" I asked a friend of mine who was curious about my camming.

"Ugh, yes!" she replied.

"Well, when I'm camming and doing an exclusive show for a femboy, or a guy who loves SPH or being humiliated in general or degraded, I think about all the men who have treated me like garbage. All the guys who ghosted me and never had the common decency to tell me they weren't interested anymore."

I mean, as a woman, I tend to overthink things. And after my second divorce, when I started dating, I had never experienced ghosting—so each time I was ghosted, it made my mind crazy. Constantly evaluating everything in the relationship. Wondering if I wasn't smart, pretty, funny, or interesting enough. Being ghosted is infuriating.

On a related note, I watched a show/documentary on Netflix called *Hot Girls Wanted: Turned On.* Episode 2

was interesting as well as enlightening. Titled "Love Me Tinder," it's about a 40-year-old fuckboy named James who lives in Las Vegas and ghosts girls when he gets bored with them. He is very candid and honest in the episode, and the epitome of a fuckboy: the kind of guy who will tell you what you want to hear in the beginning, but then, because he has 50 different dating profiles, will drop you for whoever he believes is the next best thing, a new flavor of the week. He ghosts the girls because he feels it is "too much for him to deal with" by just telling them he is no longer interested, and they are left wondering what happened.

Once I saw this, it made sense as to why I never heard again from some of the men I dated. I chalk it up to pure laziness. If you don't pay attention to it, it will go away— that is their thought process. And you know what? It worked. At least for me it did. I never beg for a man, nor will I continue to waste my time blowing up his phone. They were just pathetic little trolls who couldn't handle being upfront and honest.

The worst are those who are narcissistic sociopaths and think they can get any woman they want. They will gaslight you, meaning they will turn an argument around on you and make you feel like you are the crazy one or the one at fault. They fail to take any responsibility for their actions. They lie without a conscience, will

wear you down, and will deny things despite you having proof. Yeah, those guys ... when I'm doing SPH, I think about them, their ways, and how much they hurt me, how much they betrayed me, how many times they have lied to me—and then the verbiage just flows. It's as though I finally have the courage to say what is on my mind, but in front of a complete stranger who is enjoying it and getting off from it.

Meanwhile, as I explained all this, my friend's eyes grew huge, and she laughed so hard at what I was telling her. "I want to make them feel worthless, useless, and let them know they are not worthy to even be considered a man." My friend could completely understand and relate to where I am coming from. If these guys want brutal, then they came to the right cam girl. If they are dumb enough to pay me to belittle them, then that is their prerogative.

"A lot of men enjoy a woman in power. They find it to be a huge turn-on to be treated like a little bitch," I explained to her. There are some seriously submissive men out there. I honestly had no idea, since I have never dated a submissive guy, nor have I been friends with a true submissive type. Quite frankly, a submissive guy for me is a serious turn-off, but it makes a cam session rather enjoyable and amusing, because degrading and verbally abusing them is making me money!

PRO TIP #10

As women, we put up with a lot of bullshit from men—
sexual harassment, cat-calling, getting eye-fucked, etc.
The last thing you want to do is deal with their shit online.
Don't be afraid to call them out if they are being rude or
harassing you. Additionally, don't be afraid to kick them
out of your chat room and block them.
You can also report them to the company,
and they can ban them from ever entering the website. I'm at the point now
where I do not give second chances.
Personally, I don't even acknowledge
them anymore. I simply hit the button
to kick them out and then immediately
block them from contacting me. Some
of them thrive off getting under your
skin. I refuse to give in to that shit. Not
worth my time or energy.

CHAPTER 11

I COULDN'T
MAKE THIS UP

contemplated whether I should add this next camming
experience to this book. It could be somewhat disturbing to a lot of readers, so much so that, in the moment, I
thought, "WTF am I watching?" After discussing it with
some people close to me who have been reading tidbits of
my book as I write, they brought up the "shock value" of
this one. And our society is obsessed with things shock-
ing and weird.

It was New Year's Eve, 2018. I was all glammed up
and making good money when I received a message in
open chat from a fellow I will call "Little Cummer Boy,"
and I already know the type.

"Would you like to hear a secret?" he asked me.

"Umm, sure, if you want to divulge information to me, that's on you."

Little Cummer Boy, as I dubbed him, proceeded to tell me that he loves to suck penises for women with beautiful breasts and that he had a large rubber penis in his mouth.

Of course he does, I thought to myself as I rolled my eyes. Here we go, another guy who loves shock value and to be watched. "Let me guess, you want to show me that big old cock you're sucking on, don't you?"

"Yessssss," he replied. Little Cummer Boy took me away exclusive and requested a cam-2-cam session. Once I clicked on "accept," I saw this burly, hairy man lying down naked on his stomach, on the bed, going to town on this big dildo. "Holy hell, how big is that?" I asked. "Nine inches," he typed. "So are you straight, gay, bi, or just have this fetish?" He told me he is bi, loves pussy, but loves cock in his mouth. He said it started with a cum fetish, because he loves to eat cum, which is how he started sucking cock.

Little Cummer Boy was really getting at it. I was legitimately impressed and told him that he puts most porn stars to shame. "If you show me more, I will take it all. Tell me to take the whole thing like the cocksucker I am," he told me. So I pulled down my top and exposed my breasts, and sure as shit, he deep-throated this dildo down to the balls like a champ. I don't think he even had a gag reflex.

This session was like no other session I have seen before. I got to thinking *holy shit, I wonder if I suffer from Cacospectamania!* That my friends, is the obsession of staring at something which is repulsive. Cum-eater then told me that his condom broke and that he would be right back. Puzzled, I thought, "Huh? Condom? I didn't see a condom on the dildo." Well, apparently Little Cummer Boy was wearing one while sucking the dildo and managed to break it while ejaculating into it. "When I fill my condom, I get to lick my cum out of it," he then explained. He was back on cam by then, and he showed me the broken condom.

He put on another one and laid back on his stomach to suck this monster cock. "How the hell do you get off if you aren't jerking on your cock?" I asked him. He told me that the friction from the blankets feels good, but mostly sucking the cock is what gets him off. He was really deep-throating this dildo, and the expression on my face, well—I'm sure you can imagine I was in shock.

He managed to ejaculate again, took off the condom, put it in his mouth, sucked out his own cum, and swallowed it. At one point I had to adjust my eyes so everything looked blurry, because watching Little Cummer Boy suck the condom made me a bit nauseated, but I had to appear to still be looking at him, since that is what he

is into. This kind of fetish is way out there, even for me. Although it seriously disgusted me, my curiosity continued to get the best of me, so I just had to watch in awe. Just another day at the office.

PRO TIP #11

If you need to really hustle for some cash, don't be afraid to "take one for the team," so to speak. The above scenario is a perfect example. The above session did not violate any of my "things I will not do," but the nature of it was absurd enough to be a little disturbing, even for me. Yet I knew I was making money with him. I had to keep encouraging him to keep him interested. Was it weird and uncomfortable? Hell yes, it was, but when bills need to be paid, you do what you have to do without really compromising your "will not do" list!

CHAPTER 12

RACE PLAY

Here comes yet another fetish that is apparently a popular thing nowadays. According to Urban Dictionary, the top definition for "race play" is "an avant-garde, but increasingly accepted form of sexual role play in which people of different races consensually reject all politically correctness … in favor of sexual pleasure and fulfillment." This has been a common request from men who come to my chat room. When I first started camming, a customer asked me if I did race play, and I was confused, as I did not know this was an actual fetish that turns some people on. So again, my virgin eyes had to look up "race play" and what it entails.

Especially in the times we live in now, racism is a very sensitive subject. Even in the camming world, this fetish could be construed as controversial, and the

language I have to use to explain it may be disturbing to some readers. I was certainly baffled when one of my customers wanted me to call him a "filthy nigger," as he so eloquently put it. Those words have never come out of my mouth. It was somewhat difficult for me to learn this type of roleplay. As a white woman, I have dated a vast array of men from many races and ethnicities, so for me to belittle these men based on their race seemed odd and just wrong on every level.

That being said, I wanted to learn more about the subject because I consider myself a well-rounded cam model. Of course, I have my limits, just like everyone else, but I realized that I can make decent money doing this kind of roleplay, as I am just using my words to get a guy off. Now I generally think of it as just a roleplay—using derogatory and racist terms and language, but crossing boundaries just like any other roleplay I do. This sort of roleplay seems to excite the guy because it is so taboo, and that is what makes it arousing. This isn't much different than schoolgirl/teacher, step-mom/step-son, or doctor/patient because they all involve crossing lines that aren't acceptable in the normal world.

It took me a few times doing this roleplay to understand it. Every time is a bit uncomfortable, though. I make sure I ask what race the guy is prior to starting our race play roleplay, because once in a while, you'll get

an Asian guy with a tiny dick. However, the majority of my customers who request race play are black—such as the following one, featuring a memorable customer I will call "Hank."

Brace yourselves, because this one is a doozy. While I was flirting with other guys in my open chat room, Hank asked if I do race play, to which I replied, "Of course." He told me that he likes racial humiliation and that he is a black guy with a tiny dick. "Holy hell," I thought to myself—here I am, the SPH queen, and now I have multiple reasons to humiliate him! Jackpot!

Hank then took me exclusive to start the show. He informed me that he has no limits and prefaced our session with, "Just be as mean as possible. The meaner the better." "Oh God," I suddenly thought, "what did I get myself into? How am I going to be creative and cruel enough for this guy?" I decided just to hit the ground running.

"Welcome to my room, you piece of shit nigger! You should be so lucky to be in the presence of greatness, you filthy toad!" I said to him. That apparently got him excited.

"Can you call me a nigger after each sentence?" he asked.

Oh God, how am I going to do this? I thought to myself. But what I said was, "Sure, nigger, if that's what you want."

"You only fuck niggers with BBC, don't you?"

"Fuck yes, I do, bitch! I don't want to fuck a dirty nigger like you who has a fucking baby dick! You might as

well call your dick a clit, because that's the size of it. I bet you only use two fingers to stroke your gherkin-sized cock, don't you?"

"Yes, I do! I want to watch you fuck a BBC." So I broke out my BBC dildo and teased him with it. "Aren't you jealous of this big black cock? I bet you're so jealous that you would suck it like the little bitch that you are!"

Hank went on to tell me that he has big purple lips and a big wide nose and that he drives a hoopty. He requested that I talk shit about his appearance and about how ugly he is. I called him a homo for having such a pathetic-sized cock. "You know something, nigger? You might as well just tuck that tiny clit cock up into your asshole! Just do everyone a favor and become a tranny freak! You're never going to impregnate anyone with a pathetic cock like that, so what good are you?"

"Yeaaaaaa, I love it! More, more! Tell me I'm a nasty nigger freak!" At this point, Hank wanted my face close to the camera while flipping him off and belittling him with a mean face. "You are a pathetic piece of shit, you nasty nigger! You are scum and you don't deserve to have my body. I am a white goddess and you need to bow down to me, you fucking freak tranny! You make me so fucking sick I want to vomit!"

"Yes, Goddess, tell me I am a sissy loser!"

"Nigger, you are the biggest sissy I have ever come across. The fact that you have a clit dick is proof that you are a fucking plague to society! I bet your tiny cock doesn't even produce semen, does it? Just tuck that filthy tiny nigger cock up your ass and go play in traffic!"

Our session lasted for what seemed to be about 30 minutes. At that point, Hank logged out due to having to contact customer support. This automatic logout is usually because the customer has exceeded their daily limit with regard to spending. I was pretty satisfied with our session and glad I was able to keep him entertained; however, that being said, it was quite difficult to come up with "meaner" words or phrases. Although I was saying what he wanted, I still felt a bit remorseful. It is extremely awkward for me to really get into this. In a roleplay such as this one, it can be challenging to come up with new derogatory words or sentences. I mean, it's not every day that I use racist language to excite someone. I wonder if he ended up getting off before our session ran out?

PRO TIP #12

Men love details. They want to imagine how they are making you feel or picture you getting fucked really hard by some other guy. Don't be afraid to be descriptive about things during a session. Be descriptive with what you would do to him sexually. Once in a while, I will come across a customer and all they want me to do is strip for them while describing my last sexual encounter. Of course, I embellish, and so should you if you feel it will make the session that much better. Men love dirty talk, and if this is something that is not in your area of expertise, don't feel bad. I had to research some new phrases and terminology in order to mix it up and keep it fun and interesting.

CHAPTER 13

THE GEM

Not every guy I encounter while camming is a complete freak or weirdo. There are a lot of pretty normal, everyday guys who visit the website with the hopes of finding their perfect cam model to have a little fun with. A lot of my time camming includes me having to act out some crazy fetish or roleplay that is along the meaner side. Some guys want me to use really foul language when talking dirty, while others are just quick and to the point. "Let's get you naked," I often hear as soon as some guy takes me private or exclusive. No "Hi, how are you?" or "How is your day going?"—just straight to the point, no small talk. I suspect it's because they don't want to spend a lot of money, so small talk just gets in the way.

Additionally, as a webcam model, you are putting yourself out there and are subjected to trolls. Those are

the little piss ants who are rude or say demeaning things to you, try to ruffle your feathers for some reason, and aren't worth your time and energy. Most likely it's because they got outcasted by their peers for being creepy or weird and have never gone out on a date with a real woman, or they have some sort of animosity toward women. I have only had to kick out or block a handful of rude and obnoxious guys. When a guy makes rude or demeaning comments, I don't even acknowledge them. They aren't worth acknowledging because no response is a response. I just continue chatting with the other guys in open chat, kick out and block the douchebag, and go on my merry way. Thankfully, there are some nice and genuine guys still left on this planet.

So along comes "Alex." Alex is a gentleman I encountered not too long ago. On each cam model's page, there is an option for the customer to call the model on the phone. As long as the cam model has her phone enabled to take calls, the customer can talk instead of type. The customer obviously has no idea what your real phone number is, but it's a nice option for customers who don't like to type and would rather actually speak to their model. Alex is one of those customers who uses the phone option, and I am thankful he does. Now, why would I be thankful that he calls, you ask? Well, listening to him is like listening to sexy Sam Elliott talk. Sam

Elliott is my older man-crush, and in my mind, that is who Alex shall look like. Alex is from Louisiana, is 50 years old, and has this soothing, sexy, Southern voice that just makes me melt. I swear, this man could do phone sex, he is that good.

Alex is similar to Chris. They are both in their early fifties, from the South, are very kind, sweet, and engaging, and are all about pleasing the woman no matter how long it takes. This man just gets inside my head. He is the kind of man who truly loves women and everything about them. He is very sensual. He doesn't use rude or crude language but doesn't mind a little light dirty talk. He isn't the needy type, either, nor does he ever demand anything from me.

Alex took me exclusive. Immediately, my phone rang. I, of course, called him by his regular name and told him how good it was to see him, because it had been a while!

"Oh, Angelina, you are looking so beautiful. I've missed you!"

I was wearing a soft white button-down shirt with only one button buttoned, lacy light pink panties, and white thigh-high stockings. A very comfortable and simple ensemble, and easy to take off and put back on. "You're so sweet. How have you been?" I asked him.

"I'm doing better now that I get to see you. My God, you are a sight for sore eyes."

"You're going to give me a big head if you keep talking like that," I joked with him.

"I wish I could be there to touch and tease you ever so lightly. I would start by laying you down on your stomach, and gently kiss the back of your neck while slowly caressing your back, covering every inch of your body with my mouth and hands."

At this point, I was really taking in everything he was saying to me. I started to strip down for him and to tease him slowly and erotically. He showered me with compliments, and soon I was lying naked in front of him, slowly touching myself.

"God, you make me feel so good. You make me feel like such a strong man taking care of such an amazing woman as yourself."

I, of course, turned eight shades of red. Sometimes I don't take compliments well. No matter how many compliments I receive, I still get embarrassed. But I was getting more and more excited by listening to him tell me what he would do to me. I felt completely relaxed, soaking in this man's voice while touching myself.

"You are so incredible, Angelina. I could please you all day, taking my time with you and enjoying every part of you."

He kept talking like this, deep and sexy. I am picturing this man in my head, imagining everything he is

doing to me. The intensity is real. At some point during the conversation I had a legit, intense orgasm. This does not usually happen for me. I can count on two hands how many actual orgasms I've had while camming. Most guys think they can get me off in two minutes. Not so much there, little fella—it takes a little more than just two minutes for me to get off. For some girls, it could be much easier to orgasm, but for me, I really have to be into it mentally. I need to be mentally stimulated while camming to have that kind of orgasm. Alex was clearly excited and pleased that he had gotten me off.

"Wow, that was so incredible! Watching you cum like that was beautiful," he told me.

"Well, that doesn't happen very often at all, so thank you! You just do something to me, I don't know what it is."

We continued our session, and I got him off as well. He thanked me for my time and told me he looked forward to seeing me again.

Well, that next time was the very next day. I saw Alex enter my room. "Well, well, well, look who it is!" I said to him.

"I just couldn't stay away—I had to come back to see you, and when I saw you were online, I couldn't resist." This pleased me, letting me know I had done my job well.

"I'm so happy you decided to take me away again. I had a great time yesterday during our session!" I exclaimed.

I had made yet another "regular," but this one is a gem. When I see him, I know that all I have to do is sit back and relax as he does all the "work." It is a much-needed break from the rest of the heathens online, and for the next 20 minutes, I was enjoying yet again some amazing sexy time with my Sam Elliott, which included another real orgasm.

PRO TIP #13

Don't be afraid to let your true personality shine. Of course, for roleplays, you are acting. You are a fantasy at that point. While in open chat it's okay to let your guard down a little. Some men want a fantasy woman to take away private or exclusive, while others want someone down-to-earth and real. If you are genuine, men are attracted to that. Trust me, they tell me all the time that they appreciate how honest and genuine I am with them. This is where an emotional connection can be beneficial for you. If they have a connection with you, they will be a repeat customer. They have invested themselves with you.

CHAPTER 14

THE BIG TIPPER

After the first few months of camming, I learned to be even more open-minded with the roleplays. I would do or act out the strange fetishes some of these guys were into. I really wanted a broad array of customers in order to maximize my income and popularity.

Some cam models have absolutely no limits, and that is their choice. There is no point in doing something you are not comfortable doing, because it will show all over your face. Guys want you to be into it as much as they are! Of course, there are times where I have to embellish my enthusiasm, but I still maintain *some* enthusiasm. For me, my limits are no anal, no DP (double penetration), no mommy roleplays (sorry, I am not into incest), and no deep throat, as I have a pretty sensitive gag reflex.

I also will not let a dom attempt to abuse me in any way. I prefer to be the dominant one, but once in a while, a dom will come into my room and ask me to be his sub. Before I agree, we have to discuss the terms. I have let only one or two men act as a dom with me. I suppose that me being a dom ensures that I am the one in control, not the men, and I prefer it that way. Also, the really extreme roleplays, as mentioned earlier, are something I don't care to do. They require too much work, and some are too weird for me to even try to get into.

A new customer who goes by the screen name "Jerry" asked me while in open chat if I do race play and if I had a BBC dildo. I told him yes, and he immediately took me exclusive.

"I want to jack off my chink dick to that BBC while you be a dirty white slut who likes big nigger dicks," he typed.

"Okay, Jerry, I would love for you to watch me fuck this BBC while you're over in the corner jerking off your pathetic cock."

"I just have to jack off my little four-inch Korean dick and watch you suck and fuck that nasty nigger dick. You are a bad girl!" he said. "If I was your little gook boyfriend, you'd be sucking and fucking those nigger dicks and telling them how much bigger they are than your Asian boyfriend, telling them that you need it." I lubed up

"Tell that nasty nigger to fuck you in front of your chink boyfriend," he went on. "You think you can let him pound you like a dirty whore for $100.00? You think you can take it rough?" he asked.

"Fuck yes, I can, Jerry!" And as soon as I started pounding myself, I told him that he could never fuck me like this BBC does, and in came the $100.00 tip. Of course, he wanted to see me cum, so I faked yet another orgasm because, at that point, it had been 20 minutes of constant pussy-fucking and there was no way I would be getting myself off. Jerry was beside himself.

"I came so good. Thanks for playing kinky, baby. You have a good night."

I bade him goodnight and sat on my bed in a state of shock. I had just gotten tipped $250.00! Overall, he spent just over $400.00 for 26 minutes.

Now, sadly, I did not get to keep the entire amount of the tip, because of course both the studio and website get their cuts of my money; I only kept $50.00 of that tip. Yes, it is shitty; yes, it is not fair; but there is nothing anyone can do. I could raise my rates so I keep more of the money, but as it stands, my rates are average, and I don't want to go higher for fear I may lose out on my regulars. And thanks to Jerry, I made $116.00 in just two hours of work, so overall, I couldn't complain.

I wondered what he does for a living to have that much disposable income. I mean, to drop that much money in 26 minutes was absurd to me. Oh well—there was no point on dwelling on that. I was done for the night, as I'd had enough pussy-pounding for one night.

CHAPTER 15

THE TRIED AND TRUE: THE REGULAR

I n almost two years of camming on a pretty consistent basis, I have gained a lot of loyal customers whom I am very grateful for. They always try to make an appearance in my chat room, even if it's in open chat to say hi when they don't have time to take me away for a private session. I also make it known that I appreciate them coming by just to say hello. They made the effort, so I can respect that. I look at my regulars the way a bartender looks at their regulars. You've seen them countless times. You know each person's name, you know exactly what their poison is, and you have it waiting for them before they take a seat.

The regulars are the ones who don't cause drama. They love routine and never deviate from it. They are

always a pleasure to see, and it is effortless. No critical thinking involved. That is Pete. Pete has been a favorite of mine since I started camming. Pete is a bit of a submissive and enjoys face-sitting. Initially, Pete would ask me to sit at the edge of my chair or bed and grind my vagina as though I am grinding it on his face, suffocating him and ignoring him at the same time. He loved it when I would ignore him and would encourage me to be on my phone during our session. "Wait a minute," I said to him, "you mean to tell me you *want* me to ignore you?"

"Yes, feel free to text your friends or email while you're sitting on my face," he replied. *Did I just win the lotto? I don't have to pay this guy any attention?* I thought. Most men *need* attention and thrive off it. Hell, this guy is simple. During our sessions, he would tell me that he needs to come up for air, and he wants me to tell him to "shut up and just take it."

The other day Pete dropped by. I was dressed in a soft white button-up shirt with the sleeves rolled up and only one button buttoned. I was, of course, sporting thigh-high stockings—purple with a matching purple thong.

"Hello, Goddess," Pete said to me upon entering my open chat room.

"Pete! It's good to see you again! You came at the perfect time! It's contest week and if I place within the top 200, I earn bonus money, and I need to hustle!"

"Oh, great! Are you ready to have your pussy worshipped?" Pete asked me.

"Of course I am, Pete! You know how much I enjoy sitting on your face and suffocating you!" The good thing about Pete is that he gets right to business. He doesn't feel it's necessary for small talk while in open chat, as he knows that a lot of times I get taken away to go exclusive quickly, and then he's lost his chance. Either he waits for me to get out of exclusive or comes back another day. Today was a bit different for Pete, though, but only ever so slightly. Pete wanted the "full effect" of my vagina.

"Can you place the cam on the floor and either squat or sit at the edge of your bed so I can view your pussy from above? It will feel as though you are really sitting on my face," he explained.

"Sure, let me see what I can do," I replied. I took my webcam off of my laptop and placed in on my floor, trying to figure out the damn angle. I was viewing the cam on my end on my computer screen while simultaneously trying to angle it correctly so my frickin' vag wasn't upside down. I swear I looked like a bumbling idiot trying to figure this out. It's not complicated, so I blame the couple of vodka sodas I had as an excuse to make me feel better about myself and that I'm not a complete moron. I finally got to a place where my vagina and cam were facing the correct direction. *Jesus,* I thought to myself, *my vagina is*

seriously on display. I mean it is right up in there, full fucking frontal like I'm about to sit right on his face! The last time anyone was this close to my vagina was at my gynecologist's office, and I wasn't the one getting paid!

"Oh my God, that is perfect! Just like that!" Pete exclaimed. "I love it when you suffocate me and sit on my face!"

So I began doing my thing, grinding and sitting on the edge of my bed, a foot away from the cam, and I thought, *so I guess this is what it's like to be a straight guy or a lesbian? Yeah, no thanks. Not my cup of tea.* To each their own. As I sat there scrolling on my phone on social media, laughing and ignoring Pete, he typed, "Oh no, can't breathe, need air."

"Shut the fuck up, Pete. You don't need air, you need to continue to worship me!" I glared down at him with my most disgusted facial expression. "Stop being such a little bitch and deal with it."

"Yes, Goddess, please continue to ignore me." I laughed at his response and continued to do as he liked.

"I need to come up for air, Goddess, please!"

"Ugh, fine." I barely got up from my perch at the edge of my bed, then told him that was enough air. "Okay, that's all you get." *I'm such a bitch.* I then got off my bed and decided to squat far down to the camera on the floor so he would get the full experience of my face-sitting. I mean, I

had to tease him a little bit and get him worked up before he could get the full experience, right? Now I was squatting right over my cam. All there was to see on the cam video was vagina. I'm sorry, but I don't find anything remotely lovely or attractive about the vagina, but apparently Pete does, and he continued to tell me he couldn't get enough of my face-sitting. I'd been squatting for a few minutes at that point. My legs were starting to burn and shake a little. *Fuck, I was not expecting to get in a workout with this guy.*

"Yessssss, Goddess, thank you! I finished, that was awesome! Can you have the camera like that from now on?" he asked.

"I'm glad you enjoyed the session, and of course I can do that for you! Especially now that I know how everything needs to be set up for you to get the full-on experience! Until next time."

Pete left my room happy as a clam. As for me, I could go the rest of my life never having to see my vagina up close and personal like that ever again.

CHAPTER 16

THE STRAP-ON

A few months into camming, all of a sudden I was constantly getting asked if I had a strap-on. I thought to myself, "Why would a guy ask this?" Well, I got to thinking about it and I noticed some of the tags these guys would leave on my camming profile page: "brutal SPH," "CFNM femdom," "humiliatrix," and "SPH champ," to name a few. For those who are not familiar with CFNM femdom, it means "clothed female, naked male." When my femboys come to my room to play, they have no real interest in me doing a striptease or seeing me with my clothes off. It's a common theme in female domination or femdom scenarios. CFNM helps emphasize a guy's vulnerability and submission. Their goal is to be humiliated, to be tortured in the sense of erotic teasing, to receive a little pain, or to be deprived from touching themselves or from

cumming. It all made sense to me now! These femboys want me to simulate fucking them with my strap-on! This, apparently, is a huge turn-on for them.

One day, while sitting at the airport with some friends for a long weekend, I just happened to mention to one of my girlfriends what I do on the side. I don't quite remember how the conversation came up, but we started talking about strap-ons, how I don't have one, and how I keep forgetting to buy one. It just isn't one of those things that comes to mind when I am buying my toys or lingerie. A few minutes went by, and she asked me for my address.

"Why do you need my address?" I asked her.

"Because I'm buying you a strap-on. Do you need lube or toy cleaner?"

"Girl, are you nuts? Why are you buying me a strap-on?"

"Because your customers want you to have one. Think of it as an investment. I am investing in your project."

"You're killing me," I laughed. "Thank you, though. That's very thoughtful of you."

A few days later, I received an Amazon package in the mail. Hooray! My strap-on! I opened the box and inside was a very pretty gift bag, along with extra lube and toy cleaner. I just shook my head. "This bitch," I said to myself while laughing.

I took it out of the bag. I opted for a purple cock because I wanted it to be racially neutral. Some guys want

a black cock, others a white one, so to make my life easier, I chose the purple one because it's my favorite color. That being said, the straps looked really, really large. I tried putting it on, but I was having a total blonde moment. "Why the fuck are these straps made so long? This isn't fitting right," I grumbled to myself. *Oh well,* I thought, *I'll figure it out later.*

That Saturday night, I wore a sheer black top for my evening of camming. It had no buttons, so I tied it toward the bottom. I also wore a black, barely-there G-string and, of course, black thigh-highs. Someone new came into my chat room and asked if I have a strap-on. We will call him "Bruno"—the client, that is, not the strap-on!

"Well, Bruno, yes. I actually *do* have a strap-on. However, my friend just bought it for me and I'm not sure how to wear it right."

"I can take you private and try and help you," he said. What a gentleman!

"Oh, that would be so awesome of you, Bruno," I said. "Thank you!"

So Bruno took me private. "Okay, use the straps like underwear and stick your legs in them," he explained.

"Okay, but why does this shit look like this?" I asked him.

"I think it was made for a much larger woman," he replied.

"Ugh, for fuck's sake. Okay, I'll tighten it all the way to the last hole."

I felt like I looked like a fucking idiot trying to figure out what strap goes where and fiddlefucking around with it. *Fuck it,* I thought. *He's paying me for my time, so that's all that matters.* I finally got to the point where I believed I had it on as good as it was going to get.

"Yeah, that's it," he said. "It looks okay to me. I like it!" And immediately Bruno took me exclusive.

"You're beautiful. I have a fantasy," he said.

Jesus H. Christ, what in the name of all that is holy was I about to get into with this guy? *All* of the things were running through my head. My mind frantically scrolled through all the outlandish roleplays I'd done in the past to potentially prepare myself. But I just said, "Okay, what is it?"

"Will you dance to a specific song with the strap-on on?"

"Of course I can. What song do you want?"

"'Short Dick Man' by Gillette," he said.

I laughed out loud so hard! It brought me back to my high school days when that song came out. It depicts women mocking the size of a man's penis. A funny fact about the song: the artists figured there were all these songs by men bashing women and treating them like sex objects, so they decided that a song that turned the tables on men might attract some attention. I hadn't heard this song in what felt like a hundred years, since around 1994!

I went to YouTube to find the song. Bruno proceeded to tell me that he is a "sub bottom," which, for those not familiar with that term, is the person in gay sex who lets his partner do whatever he pleases during sex and usually prefers doggy-style or knee-bender sex positions. Bruno also wanted me to make tiny-cock gestures using my hand when the words "Short Dick" were said during the song.

"Okay, Bruno, let's do this!"

As the song began, I was on my bed kneeling, dancing, and simulating fucking him from behind while making my small-cock hand gestures. Actually, the strap-on didn't look as bad as I expected. *This could totally work*, I thought.

"Bend over, bitch, and take it like the little slut you are, Bruno!" I shouted, thrusting my hips.

"That is great, I love it! Fuck me, baby! Use that cock!" he told me. I was feeling so nostalgic at this moment, listening to this song, remembering laughing with all my girlfriends in high school and blasting the song every time it came on the radio. At this point I was really giving it to him and telling him to shut the fuck up and let me have my way with him. Inside my head, I was giggling because this was so silly to me. Across from my bed is a big mirror attached to my dresser, so I could see myself simulating fucking this guy with this strap-on. I really looked ridiculous, but this is what the customer wanted, and since it didn't violate any of my limits, screw it. Did

I look like a moron doing this? Sure, but it kept the customer happy and I was getting paid!

Sadly, Bruno said goodbye and thanked me before the song ended. I guess he came rather quickly, so not only did he most likely have a tiny cock, but he was a fast cummer to boot. This guy had no hope. Oh well—another satisfied customer, and a new toy that I hoped will bring me more laughs and more money!

PRO TIP #14

For those who are interested in webcamming, research your sites. There are a lot of webcam sites out there. I did not know this when I first started. When I replied to the Craigslist ad and met up with the studio manager, that was when she told me what cam site they are affiliated with. The site is one of the more reputable and popular sites and has been around for some time. It's well-designed and easy to navigate. The company I work for has a huge range of performers, from amateurs to professional porn stars, and provides plenty of high-definition and live-audio-streaming cams. There is always a huge selection of models online, which can easily be filtered by fetishes, categories, and types. The site also offers customers suggestions for performers that closely match their criteria. You're bound to find a site that meets your needs.

CHAPTER 17

THE SWITCH HITTER

I came across "Vick" when I first started camming. He had been a long-time regular with me, so it was always a pleasure to see him when he entered my chat room. Vick has always been nice and respectful toward me, but he has a fetish that none of my other customers have. You see, Vick likes to switch it up every now and again, but only between two specific roleplays. They are always the same, so I know what he's looking for.

When I first encountered Vick and he told me what he's into, I wasn't sure if I wanted to do it, but after a while I realized it's more about the behavior I portray for this particular roleplay. You see, Vick … well, he likes it when I act out as a bratty 14-year-old girl who has never had sex before, and Vick is my mentor. Essentially, he tells me what to do while I act bratty and naïve.

I know what some of you may be thinking—that this guy is a dirty pervert who likes to screw young girls. No, that is not the case with this particular customer. He enjoys it when I act like I am pouting or bossy. Then, on the flip side, Vick will have his days where he wants me to show him why a 40-year-old woman is better than a 14-year-old girl. What he wants depends on the day and his mood. One day, as I was sitting in one of my black "come fuck me" outfits (a black body stocking, to be exact), Vick entered my open chat.

"Well, well, look who it is!" I said to him.

"Hey, Angelina, it's been a while! How have you been?"

"Oh, busy as usual," I replied.

"Well, you know what I want, so how about I take you exclusive?" he asked.

"Yes, please, before I die of boredom sitting in open chat!"

Vick then took me away exclusive. Naturally, I was wondering which character he wanted me to play today.

"I want you to show and tell me why you are better than a 14-year-old," he told me.

"First of all, no 14-year-old little slut is going to have a rack like mine, Vick. Come the fuck on. You would have a field day motorboating my boobs and tit-ty-fucking me!" I explained, while slowly taking off my body stocking to show just my breasts, teasing him in front of the camera.

was saying this to him, I shook and spanked my ass, hoping I was making his cock throb.

"I love your big, round ass and all your curves. No 14-year-old would have your kind of body," he told me.

"Thank you, Vick. I'm glad I got you convinced that a 40-year-old woman is by far better than some 14-year-old little bimbo!" I then started to fuck myself with my dildo. "No 14-year-old can take a cock-pounding, Vick. It's just never gonna happen. Only a real woman, such as myself, can handle quite the pounding and enjoy it!"

Meanwhile, I continued to fuck myself for the next 30 seconds or so, and then my show ended. I heard the sound that indicated he had left the session. Since I had my back to the computer screen, I didn't realize Vick was that excited.

"*Wow!* I just came so fucking hard! That was awesome, Angelina! Thank you!" I read on the screen. Despite our session not being very long, I was satisfied that I had convinced Vick that an older woman is where it's at!

CHAPTER 18

THE KARDASHIAN SYNDROME

You may be wondering why on earth I would name a chapter after the Kardashians. Well, here's the reason: sometimes when camming, I come across men who don't require me to do much of anything. No changing, no dirty talk, no dancing, no shifting to different sex positions or moving to other rooms. Let me tell you, this is a welcome break! When you are constantly "on" all the time, it gets exhausting. When I say "on," that means interacting, roleplaying, dildo-sucking, pussy-fucking, etc. In these shorter sessions, I essentially feel like a Kardashian because I am getting paid to do nothing.

One day, quite some time ago, a gentleman by the name of "Ira" stopped into my open chat room and took me exclusive pretty much right away. As we began the

cam-2-cam session, I saw this older gentleman with glasses sitting in a rather dark room. I welcomed Ira into my room. Ira wasn't much of a conversationalist. All he wanted me to do was sit really close to my cam and open my mouth wide as he examined my mouth and teeth. Of course, you can imagine the look on my face when this was all he requested from me. Are you familiar with the "Side-Eye Chloe" meme? If not, I suggest you look it up in order to understand my facial expression, and for those who are familiar, that look was me! If I'm not mistaken, I think Ira used to be a dentist back in the day.

Anyway, Ira told me how to position my mouth so he could observe all my teeth. As I was doing this, I watched him move his glasses up and down during these observations of his. He told me to open my mouth big and wide like a huge yawn, and he complimented my teeth. I am blessed with straight teeth and I've only had two cavities, so my mouth isn't filled with black holes or anything. He found it intriguing that I've only had two cavities, asked me to yawn wide a couple more times, and thanked me. I think the session lasted less than five minutes. But again, I got paid for doing nothing.

"Ryan" is a frequent regular of mine and has an ass fetish. He's not much for small talk, but a little more than Ira, although he does compliment me more and says hi. Ryan is really into anal gaping. What is that, you ask?

Well, it is the act of having extended anal sex with the goal of opening up the anus wide for a period of time. After having anal sex, the next step would be to put progressively larger items into your anus. It is probably the most extreme form of anal stretching. As you know, doing anything anal for me is a no-go. With this particular customer, though, he doesn't take it to an extreme level. All Ryan wants is for me to bend over, ass close to the camera, and spread my ass cheeks as much as I can.

"I could spend hours eating your ass," he said to me.

"I'm sure you could, Ryan, you little freak," I replied. All the time I was thinking, what makes an asshole so alluring? You wouldn't catch me tossing some guy's salad, i.e., performing anilingus. Not on my watch—it's just not my thing.

But Ryan had a different opinion altogether. "Your ass is so round and juicy. I fucking love it!"

I grabbed a pillow to rest my head on while spreading my ass as wide as possible for him. At one point, I caught myself dozing off! I quickly looked back at my computer screen to see if he had written anything else to me. He was ready to cum, and I encouraged him to shoot his load all over my ass. He thanked me for our session, and we said our goodbyes. I sat and thought, *Wow, is this a thing? Guys will spend $5.99 a minute to jerk off to me spreading my ass cheeks so they can look at my butthole?* Different strokes for different folks!

"Peter" was a new customer who I recently encountered. He took me away exclusive. He is a chatty one, which can be nice because it alleviates me having to be creative and think of things to talk about. He greeted me and asked how I was doing.

"I'm okay," I told him, "but I was so bored sitting there in open chat, and nobody was really interacting with me, so thank you for taking me exclusive! How are you?"

"I'm good, thanks for asking. At least now you have better use of your time. Why chat for free?"

"I know, right? So what are you up to, Peter?"

"Wife is taking a nap right now," he told me.

"Oooohh, Peter, you naughty boy! Your wife is taking a nap and you come online to get naughty with me? I love it! Where is she and where are you?" I asked him with enthusiasm. I just love it when men have girlfriends or wives but would rather pay me to entertain them!

"I'm in my office upstairs and she is downstairs. Would you kindly show me your pussy? My wife has been denying me lately. She has been using a strap-on on me."

I laughed at him, got myself comfortable on my bed, and began by slowly taking off just my G-string before spreading my legs open for him in front of the camera.

"How unfortunate for you, Peter. Have you been able to get off at all?" I asked him.

"Sometimes, but not always. I've only gotten to cum at

strip clubs and while online. My wife has been training me to be her little bitch. She now calls my asshole a pussy and my dick a clit." As Peter was explaining all his woes to me, I just sat back and did nothing except laugh at him. *Holy shit, this one is easy! Not only do I NOT have to do shit but lay here with my vag on display, but I don't even have to come up with a topic for conversation,* I thought to myself. I think the Kardashians should adopt me.

"So why does she call your dick a clit?" I asked him.

"It *is* a clit, since it doesn't fuck pussy and it gets wet with a dildo inside me. My wife tells people she has a 'sad' sex life. She says she prefers a vibrator to my clit." I often wonder if the stories these guys tell me are true or not. I go with it, though, because it makes it more entertaining for me in situations like this one, as I continue to do nothing but sit there.

"God, Peter, you really need to step up your game."

"I even came in my pants during a lap dance last weekend," he told me.

"What the fuck, Peter! Seriously? So what did the dancer do? Did she see anything?"

"She laughed and asked for a big tip. Honestly, have you ever heard of that before?"

"Umm, not so much, but I'm sure horny losers such as yourself do jizz in their pants at strip clubs because you all get too excited and can't control yourselves."

He nodded. "I sat there alone, wet, cold, and ashamed of myself."

"As you should, Peter, as you should. You had to do a pathetic walk of shame to your car, too, and you didn't even get laid! I expect more from you, Peter." All of a sudden, I got a "thank you" from him as he left my room. He must have gotten off. All I needed was that silly "That was easy" button from Staples to end my show!

Once in a while, I encounter a guy who just *has* to be watched. They are usually full of themselves and love voyeurism. These types of sessions are quick, but again, I don't have to do shit but sit there. No energy is required on my end. "Allen" is one of these, and he swings by once in a while. It had been some time since I had seen him, and I looked forward to his visit when he made an appearance again. I welcomed him to my room when he entered.

"Do you want to watch me jerk my cock while eating yogurt?" he asked. Here comes that Side-Eye Chloe again.

"Sure, I would love to watch that!" I said eagerly. I was relieved because I needed a break to do nothing but sit and get paid. I had been belittling people and fucking myself with my toys for hours, so I was mentally and physically drained. Allen immediately took me away and requested a cam-2-cam session. I accepted, and then immediately saw him completely naked from far away. He ensured his

entire body was in the camera shot. He had a great body and a good-sized cock as well, both of which I complimented him on. He was well-defined but not too muscular. His cock appeared to be a solid eight inches. I've gotten good at judging cocks. (Yes, that is a thing sometimes. Men will take you away just so you can judge their cock and guess their size. Again, nothing is required on my end but to sit and judge.)

And he was stroking his cock like a madman. That thing was hard as a rock! He then reached over, took a huge handful of what appeared to be yogurt from a bowl on the counter, rubbed it all over his cock, and returned to stroking. *What the fuck is the point of that?* I wondered. Is this some new-age lube idea that the millennials are using now? Whatever works for you, my friend.

He then switched hands to jerk his cock and with his other hand, reached over to the yogurt again, and started just eating it right from the bowl. Wow … this was a first for me. I've never seen anyone enjoy yogurt as much as this guy did. Sitting on my bed, completely clothed and watching this guy yank on his cock like it's his last jerk-off session, made me giggle. This guy's face was so intense. It baffles me that someone gets so turned on by simply having me watch him jerk off. Maybe it was my facial expressions that excited him, because I have *no* poker face and have actually need to work really hard to create one

at times. But fuck! When I see shit I'm not prepared for, those facial expressions have a mind of their own.

About a minute or two later, Allen ended our session. I couldn't determine if he got off or not because of all the damn yogurt covering his dick, but I assume he did. Good for you, Allen, and thank you for the much-needed break!

CHAPTER 19

DO I DETECT A HINT OF MINT?

So there I was, just another Saturday afternoon camming, sporting some lovely pink thigh-highs bought for me by my submissive and most loyal fan, Ed. Of course, he came by my open chat to say hi and to see what stockings I was sporting that day. He was pleased with his purchase and wondered when I would have a guy in my life shoot his load on the stockings for him. I told him to just be patient and that my friends with benefits will need to know what they are getting into now that the boyfriend is out of the picture. A few of my regulars came by, but none of my favorites, Ed being the only exception. It was looking like a relatively dull camming day. Dull days are the absolute worst. I end up sitting in open chat much longer than I want, essentially twiddling my thumbs. The

guys weren't overly engaging with me, and it's like pulling teeth to get some interaction. Sitting there not talking makes me anxious. I can't stand the silence.

But then along came Pierre. He was new to my room and asked me how dominant I am.

"Well, it depends on what you're into. Every sub has their limits or specifics. I can humiliate, make you use a butt plug, make you use nipple clamps, simulate spanking or whipping you, peg you with my strap-on, force you into a simulated glory hole. The possibilities are endless."

"I enjoy all of that!" he exclaimed. "I would like you to change into a different outfit, though," he replied. *Ugh*, I thought. Most times I hate changing, as it requires me to put in more effort and takes up time. Typically, when a guy asks me to change outfits, I change and within three minutes he leaves my show. It can be frustrating, especially when I have to tear my closet apart to find certain clothing items.

"Okay, well, what do you want me to change into?" I asked him.

"I want you to put on a tight pair of jeans with boots and a shirt or tank top that is tight and will make your tits push up. I also want you to wear a belt, but I would like to choose it." *Shit, that is easy. But why is he into belts?* I thought.

"Yeah that is no problem, I have all of those items."

Pierre then took me exclusive. I told him I would be

right back so I could change. He asked me to bring out all my belts so he could make a selection. I grabbed a pair of stretchy skinny jeans, then put on my black knee-high boots and a strappy, tight pink tank top. I grabbed my plethora of belts and headed back to my bed, showing them all off and describing them to him. He selected a thick black leather belt with rhinestones that he wanted me to wear loosely—think circa 1980s. He then wanted me to keep out a brown leather belt with steel studs on it—think biker babe. Next he requested a cam-2-cam session, which I accepted. There he was, full frontal, jerking his cock for me. Pierre instructed me to make him do anything I wanted, to be as mean as I wanted, and to move from my bed to the floor so he could view my entire outfit. I moved my laptop and stood over to the side of my bed so he could get a full view.

"Looks like I got you all sorts of excited, you pathetic fucking toad! You make me sick! You got too hard too quick! Why don't you flick your pathetic cock for getting hard so quickly!" I yelled at him.

Sure as shit, there he went, flicking his dick right in front of me. Although the cam-2-cam session had no sound, I could tell by the expression on his face that all of this dick flicking was a bit painful. I took my belt and simulated spanking his ass with it by whipping it against my bed post for effect.

"Take that, bitch! That's what you get for being a dirty filthy whore!" I shouted. At some point the video on his end froze up. *Oh hell, I hope this doesn't screw up our session.* About 30 seconds later his video started streaming again, only at this point I could see him there, cock still hard—but now he had something wrapped around his neck!

What the fuck? I got closer to my screen to try and get a better look at what was around his neck. It looked like a necktie at first. He was literally choking himself out!

"What the hell do you have around your neck?" I asked him. "It looks like a necktie or stockings. Wait ... wait a fucking minute ... is that a belt?"

He typed back "belt," and I was a bit taken aback. Now I understood his fixation with belts. Yeah ... I did not see that one coming. Watching this guy jerk his cock in one hand while choking himself with a belt simultaneously is a bit alarming, to put it mildly. I watched curiously, wondering how far he would take this. Would he pass out on me from asphyxiation? (For those of you who are wondering what my facial expression was, feel free to Google the "total shock guy meme." It's one of the first memes that pops up.)

Oh, but wait ... there's more. Pierre reached over and grabbed a tube of something that I assumed was lube. Here's the thing in camming. Don't ever assume. Pierre squeezed whatever was in the tube all over his hand and cock and

started stroking himself again. It was white in color and very thick-looking. Not lube, not lotion. Wait a sec …

"What the fuck is all over your cock? It looks like toothpaste. Are you using toothpaste to masturbate with?" I asked him in disbelief.

He typed, "yes, toothpaste." Well, this was a new one for me. He stopped choking himself for the moment so he could use his other hand. All the while, I kept thinking how that toothpaste must be burning his pee-hole and how sticky it looked. At this point, I was not doing much of anything because I was curious as to what he was going to do next. And I was in for another surprise. He put toothpaste on his other finger and started fingering his butthole.

How can that be pleasurable? I thought. Well, that is one way to keep your butthole fresh for tossing salads. Pierre finished at some point, and our session ended with him thanking me. I sat and thought to myself, I wonder if he was using whitening toothpaste. *Perhaps he's a bit of a diva and wanted his asshole to be bleached, and if so, that is one economical way to go!*

CHAPTER 20

LIVING MY DOUBLE LIFE

L iving a double life (so to speak) can get exhausting after a while. I wish I had the balls to announce to the world what I do on the side, but at this point in my life, I can't risk losing my day job. I also couldn't stand the shock, criticism, and possible ostracism from my conservative family. If strangers or people I don't have a close relationship with want to judge me, then fine. They play no major role in my life and they don't affect me. If I am not harming myself or others, then why the fuck do people care? Well, everyone thinks their opinions are the right opinions. My family would never understand my position as to why I started webcamming in the first place. I have family members who are somewhat intrusive and overbearing and need to know everyone's business. Being a

private person in general, I have issues with people being too invasive. Thankfully (knock on wood), I haven't let anything slip in any conversations I've had with them.

"What are your plans this weekend?" a family member texted me.

What the hell? Are you serious right now? I thought to myself. It was a Tuesday at eight in the damn morning, and Side-Eye Chloe was making her appearance again. The previous weekend had just ended, and I didn't even know what I was having for lunch, never mind about my upcoming weekend plans. The only time I know in advance what my plans are for the weekend is if I'm going on a trip. I have to lie and make up excuses about what I'm doing if I plan on camming over the weekend. I stopped what I was doing at work and frantically tried to think of a believable excuse that she wouldn't ask too many questions about.

"I'm getting together with Dianna. She needs a wine night and a venting session with me. Our schedules just haven't meshed, so now we finally have a chance to get together," I told her.

That seemed to satisfy her curiosity, and she dropped the subject. *Fuck*, I thought. That alleviated my anxiety just a bit. Weekends are my bread and butter, especially if I *have* to cam to pay a bill, or if something went wrong with my car.

Hell, not long ago another family member offered to do my taxes for me. Yes, I know most taxes are easy to do with Turbo Tax and Tax Act; however, when I see numbers, I become anxious and I panic. But there was no way I was going to let one of my relatives see my 1099 contractor form and get all nosy, asking for details about what industry my part-time job is in and where these tips are coming from. Fortunately, I already have a tax guy, who happens to be a good friend and takes away all my number anxiety every year. He's been doing taxes forever, has owned multiple homes and businesses, and I trust him. He reached out to me again this year to see if I needed his help. I sure did—but all of this was going to take some delicate handling.

First, I told my family member that I have investments and that my tax guy knows how to handle all that stuff. I had to be quick on my feet to come up with a believable excuse, but it worked! Yet now I had to explain to my tax guy about my illustrious career as a webcam model. "Okay," I texted him, "before you do my taxes for me this time, I have to tell you something. You may think of me in a negative way."

"Lol, OK … what is it?" he replied.

"Well … I'm a webcam model," I texted back with the emoji of the monkey putting its hands over its eyes. That, I feel, is the universal emoji for being embarrassed.

"Oh wow, really? I thought you were going to tell me you're an escort," he texted.

I laughed. "So you don't think any less of me?"

"Not at all, it's your life. Do what makes you happy," he told me.

Whew, that was a huge relief! A big weight had been lifted off my shoulders. He was someone I have always been pretty transparent with, though, and that is something he appreciates. Of course, when he came over to do my taxes, he had all sorts of questions, which I didn't mind answering. He found my alter ego a bit intriguing and was amused when I told him some of my camming-session stories.

I decided that this year I would be redecorating my apartment. My furniture was literally falling apart and had gone through so many moves in 15 years that I felt it was time to upgrade a bit. Now, with all these big purchases, I'm waiting for a particular family member to ask how I could afford all this new furniture, especially since I have told them about all the debt I am paying off. I have paid off a considerable amount thus far, which has made it easier for me to upgrade my furniture. Granted, my finances are none of their business, but sometimes I have to provide a little information so they won't keep asking questions. The last thing this person wants to do, however, is to continue to interrogate an investigator.

I will shut your shit down real quick. Of course, I have already mastered the various excuses and explanations ahead of time.

Does this seem like a lot of work? At times, yes, but to keep the peace in my family, it is something I'm willing to do. I feel that as long as I continue to stay one step ahead of people, my secret will stay safe for now. Seriously, how the hell do people live double lives with hidden families? Sometimes I hear about those Lifetime movies about a husband who has a second spouse and kids who live in a completely different state that he goes back and forth to see. They manage to keep that shit a secret! That is way too much work for me. Hell, my double life is simpler than that mess, and I still find it difficult to constantly make up lies and excuses.

I know I don't owe anyone any explanations, but in my family, it's just easier to make shit up. At least my family lives far enough away so they can't just "drop in" whenever they feel like it. No, I am a solid 45 minutes away.

When I do have family or friends over to my place who have no knowledge of my alter ego, I have to ensure that I haven't left any of my sexual paraphernalia around. My bedroom can get out of hand at times. Lingerie thrown all over the room, heels all over the floor, sex toys, lube, etc. need to be hidden at all times. I have so much shit to stuff in my drawers that when my customers want me to

change outfits, all of it stays on my floor for a bit because I get tired of always putting it away.

Although I cam to pay off my debt, I like to be able to give my non-intrusive and non-invasive family members things that they would never give themselves—week-end getaways, spa days, or a night at a five-star hotel—because they deserve it. Seeing those family members happy makes me happy. And since I don't have children of my own, I don't mind spoiling the younger children in the family and my goddaughter. My family doesn't come from money, so being able to help brings me joy.

I know what you're thinking: why would someone who claims she has no fucks left to give, give so many fucks about keeping her after-hours life a secret? My family are very hard-headed people. Even when you explain things to them in a reasonable and logical manner, they still have their opinions, and you can't do anything to change them. It is easier to avoid confrontation because I would never hear the end of it. The fear of being ostracized will always be my biggest fear, should they ever find out my side job. It's the people I don't know, who judge me, that I give no fucks about. I do not and will not let negative people affect me. And why should I? I'm making money in a safe way, behind a camera, in the security of my own home.

I often wonder how long I will be able to keep this façade going or how long I will continue to cam. I can't

predict the future. Hell, I don't even know what I'm having for lunch today (as usual). All I know is that I can just live my best life, and surround myself with people who fuel my soul with positivity, while shaking my ass for the camera!

ACKNOWLEDGMENTS

I wrote this book on a whim. I have no experience in writing aside from a creative writing class and a lot of research papers in college. I would often share my outlandish webcamming sessions with a handful of friends whom I trusted because I couldn't keep these stories to myself. I *had* to tell people! Stella has been a good friend of mine for about five years. She is the friend I go to if I want a blunt and honest opinion. She is someone who I knew wouldn't judge me for my "extracurricular activities." After a few months of listening to me share some bizarre webcamming sessions, she encouraged me to write a book. Write a book about this stuff? Seriously? This stuff is way too weird for the mainstream audience. She told me that was a selling point—that nobody has written about the subject to this extent, and that people find the weird and bizarre fascinating. I contemplated writing for weeks as

she kept insisting, "don't think, just write." "I don't know how to write a book," I told her. "Brain dump everything, then go back and edit." She had a good point, and that is what I did.

I wanted to give readers a true and authentic look into the world of webcamming, at least from my point of view. Everyone knows sex sells. That being said, this is not your mainstream erotica novel. That was too commercial for me to write. I wanted to expose the most offbeat, grotesque, and comical webcam sessions I have encountered, but I threw in some "normal" sessions too because not all of my camming sessions are unusual or freakish. I wanted to incorporate humor and controversy in this book as well. What fun is a book without humor and controversy? People don't remember boring.

I wanted to educate readers about diverse and peculiar kinks, fetishes, and roleplays, since I had to educate myself on the subject matter. Some people may feel ashamed or embarrassed about what turns them on, but I wanted to inform them that they aren't alone. Many people share those same turn-ons. An attorney friend of mine put it to me in an interesting way. She told me that I am providing a public service. Webcamming provides a safe and private outlet for people to express their sexual desires if they feel ashamed or embarrassed to act out with a significant other, if they have one. Even if they

don't have a significant other, they still need some sort of outlet for release.

During the beginning of my journey, I started giving sample chapters to a couple of my other girlfriends to read and get their feedback. I wanted other women's thoughts and opinions and to know whether they could relate to the material. Then I got to thinking, maybe men will find this subject matter just as fascinating, so I elicited opinions from some of my guy friends and sent them a few chapters to peruse. Between all of my friends, I received a lot of great feedback that helped me write this book. Their encouraging words and constant support helped me believe in myself, and I am forever grateful for them.

This journey has been eye-opening for me. Between researching editors, graphic designers, self-publishing, and potential legal matters, it was overwhelming, but I welcomed the challenge of creating this book on my own. I hired some amazing and truly talented women to join my team. They are the epitome of professional. They are some of the most dedicated and hard-working women I have had the pleasure of working with.

I chose a team of women for a few reasons. First, I am a big proponent of women supporting women. I wanted to hire freelancers to support their careers, as they are supporting my book. Second, it was their energy, passion,

and enthusiasm that drew me to hiring them. And third, it was their overall talent. I viewed their work and was very impressed. My editor Rebecca was truly excited to work on this project with me. I was nervous to submit my requests for quotes to editors. Would they think my book was too outlandish for them to work on? Would anyone be interested? Would they judge me too harshly for wanting to write about this topic? Luckily for me, Rebecca was very intrigued and appreciated my honesty. She kept my work authentic so that my voice was still heard. Domini, my book cover and interior designer, is quite talented. She was very thorough and heavily involved with my design concept. She visualized my concepts brilliantly. And thank you to Pam from Femme Art Boudoir, who took beautiful photographs that inspired Domini to use them for my book. I thank these women for helping me bring this book to life.

To my lady friends who have been alongside me during my journey (Stella, Jami, Dee, Mari, Lo), thank you for your unconditional love, support, and for providing me your opinions, suggestions, and overall thoughts throughout this process. I truly value your friendships!

ABOUT THE AUTHOR

Eliza Wilde is the author of *Shock Value: A Cam Girl's Sexy and Hilarious Stories of Capitalizing on Sexual Desire*. Not only is she a webcam model—she's also a legal investigator, an Air Force veteran, and an artist. She has an undergraduate degree in legal studies, although after she started webcamming, she felt a degree in psychology may have been more useful. She is fascinated by psychology, sexology, and human sexuality, and she wanted to share with the world her insights about and interactions with her clients. She is known for her love of Dunkin' Donuts coffee, true-crime shows and documentaries, quality vodka, and sarcasm. When she isn't out investigating or writing her blog, she spends her time traveling, working out, brunching with friends while drinking mimosas, and binge-watching Netflix with her pit bull, Diesel.

CPSIA information can be obtained
at www.ICGtesting.com
Printed in the USA
LVHW110255300719
625691LV00028B/114/P

9 780578 525235